More Bedside Urban Voltaire

More Bedside
Urban Voltaire

Jack McLean

LOCHAR PUBLISHING · MOFFAT · SCOTLAND

For Tony Gallaher
and
Billy Kelly

Published by Lochar Publishing Limited
   MOFFAT DG10 9ED

British Library Cataloguing in Publication Data
McLean, Jack
More beside urban Voltaire
1. Humorous prose
I Title
828.91407

ISBN 0-948403-85-3

Typeset in 11pt on 13pt New Century Schoolbook
by Origination, Dunstable, Beds.
and printed by Harper Collins Manufacturing.

Contents

Foreword

I first met Jack McLean when I was working as education correspondent of *The Scotsman* in the early 70s. Not a particularly interesting job, you'd think, and you'd be right – but you did meet some interesting people, among them the "student leaders" of the day (an amazing number of whom now occupy, 20 years on, very senior positions in the Labour Party). Jack McLean was at the very end of his days as a "student leader". He had been teaching in a southside Glasgow secondary for some time but he still turned up at various student agitations. He also turned up at EIS agitations, in which he seemed to take less pleasure. Jack had an attractive personality, albeit somewhat louche and farouche, not to say crapulous and saturnine. He was a very funny talker.

In those days he was writing the odd piece for the Times Scottish Educational Supplement. These pieces were stupendously boring; there was no hint of the pyrotechnics that were to come. Jack seemed to be playing some refractory game, seeing if he could pen prose even more costive than the constipated stuff that appeared elsewhere in that most drab of journals.

A year or so later, I became features editor of *The Scotsman*. For the first time in my journalistic career, I was a commissioning editor; I could ask other people to write, rather than write myself. This soon proved to be less agreeable than it sounded, for you also had to wade through many submissions, some of them unspeakably turgid. One day Jack appeared and with, for him, unusual timidity, asked if I could possibly have a wee look at a couple of articles. I read the first piece, more out of duty than in expectation, but halfway through it I started guffawing. It was the funniest thing I had seen in many years, a perverse critique of sentimental Scottish nationalism in the form of a bitter, wildly exaggerated diatribe about a ridiculous primary schoolteacher who had distorted romantic episodes in Scottish history.

We printed it, and then another similar piece. The rest is, if not history, then the most remarkable success story in modern Scottish journalism. Jack's offerings became regular, in the form of a city diary. When Arnold Kemp became editor of *The Glasgow Herald* in 1981 Jack was the first *Scotsman* writer he took with him. Jack's writing became, if not more disciplined with the *Herald* , at least tighter – a word that has a variety of meanings. He won award after award. He continued to make us all laugh, but a new, bleaker tone often informed his work. Jack was becoming a social critic, tilting at the absurdities and the injustices and the meannesses and the pretensions of modern Scotland with a robust vigour and a rough honesty that is unequalled. Jack can write like an angel. But he steps where angels fear to tread; he steps on to our most precious illusions and stamps them into the dust. He is still very funny. But he has become an angry writer, and a great one.

Harry Reid
Deputy Editor, The Glasgow Herald

Food

Memories of Mealtimes *6th Nov. 1981*

TO AN epicure like myself, this land of ours can offer a number
of frustrations. The average restaurant is usually below it, and
no amount of reports on catering seems to do much good. I'll
tell you though, I reckon that chaps like Egon Ronay and
Derek Cooper, while being justifiably critical of Scots cuisine,
are probably unaware of one of the basic reasons for this state
of affairs. I noted the reason but recently when I ventured, for
the first time in years, into the Dinshie.

The Dinshie, as every school-child knows, is the school
dining hall. It is sometimes known as 'the dinner school,' and
though this suggests that the institution has a pedagogic slant
to its existence, devil the bit of education about food you will
get in most Dinshies.

It was just the other week that I took my courage in both
hands and braved my way into my local dining hall. A queue of
apparently starving boys and girls stood patiently as we
teachers skipped in front of the little beasts. I grasped a plate
with a piece of what looked like a surgical operation, which was
seemingly regarded as pizza pie, and proferred the plate for a
portion of chips. The dinner-lady (a truly quaint term that is!)
sneaked five chips on the plate. Five! Even I can count such a
number at a glance. I asked politely if I could have a few more.
The dinner-lady (whom I was told later was somewhat of a
legend for her severe application of both chips and education
cuts) rolled her eyes and administered the sort of shocked
expression one might have expected had I asked for sauteed
infants brains, and plenty of it. Two more chips appeared
resentfully on the white expanse of tablewear. 'Yer kiddin',' I
said in astonishment. By this time the dinner-lady was
soundlessly but artistically expressing the concept that
teachers were lucky to get a plate of thin gruel laced with an
untraceable poison which worked in seconds. After
considerable searching with the little shovel she so fiercely

9

wielded, the dinner-lady found a collection of small brown bits which measured ten millimetres by two.

The consumption of the chips I found to involve severe difficulty too. Any attempt to cut one in half was fraught with danger. The entire dining hall flew with bits of skiting chips. At every dinner table small boys and girls were having their eyes almost put out by little brown slivers flying at the speed of sound. Other children were having their tongues pierced (and not a bad idea at that) by potato splinters upon which mere molars could have little effect. In short, my last visit to the Dinshie was something of a nightmare.

Not so much a nightmare as my first visits were though. Back in the days of my youth chips were an entirely unknown comestible in the dinner schools and, in fact, food was pretty unknown too if it comes to that. There was no question of a choice between meat pies and fish and spaghetti and the Great British version of curry, all sultanas, bits of incongruous apple and overboiled rice. There was instead a meat course and a pudding.

The grub then was of such a surreal tone that Marinetti himself would have been proud of it. Where Glasgow Corporation got snake-meat from I do not know. Cabbage, an ever-present vegetable, seemed to have been used initially for an experiment in paper-making. Gravy was not based on Bisto, believe me, and I suspect that Dinshie cooks always mistook Vim for cornflour. Steak pies were pearl grey, with dashing bands of charcoal, like an Art Deco cigarette box. The filling tasted similar to that, too. It was in the 'cuisine minceur,' that the Dinshie chefs reached their highest point. The mince possessed a faint lilac hue, and tasted of long-dead flies. And the mashed potatoes were breathtaking. Clearly boiled in polluted rain-water wrung from old raincoats, they were brightly coloured in a virulent green.

Of course, given such a Scottish Colourists view of food, it was small wonder that such artistic endeavour went into the puddings. Sago like frogspawn, custard like something squeezed out of a spot, incarnadine jelly made out of used re-tread tyres and the infamous caramel cake! This last confection was greatly desired by Dinshie adherents, and queues of Polish proportions waited for second helpings of it. I could never understand this, for one's teeth were welded together in seconds by the superglue topping, and the consumption of another slice must have involved nasal ingestion.

But the whole Dinshie experience reeked of art, as the dining hall reeked of laundry. Strange Dadaistic rites were enacted from the prayers intoned by such active members of the Falange as headmasters, to the demeanor of the fourth-year lunkheads who clipped your ticket, and your ear when the teachers weren't looking. And the strangest thing of all was that there were a number of halfwits who actually liked it. I have ever since thought that the greatest insult I can bestow on a fellow human is that he is the sort of chap who always ate all of his school dinner.

I suspect that Messrs. Ronay and Cooper are in fact unaware of such introductions to our culinary tradition. They are probably unaware of the reaction of most of us to the Dinshie, which was to spend the 4/9d on five Bachelor and an hour of snooker. But I hope the foregoing might explain why so many of us Scots can play a fair game of snooker, and smoke like chimneys, and never consider the question of food at all. Except, of course, such epicures as me.

Recipes for the Very Sick   *22nd June 1984*

The Italian Futuristic poet Marinetti was a dedicated revolutionary in certain matters, even if his politics were to the right of Alan Massie. The fellow seemed to believe that, for Italy to be strong and back to the days of the Roman Empire, something would have to be done about the Eyetie diet. He was particularly scathing about the national dish of spaghetti, claiming that it was not possible to go marching on Rome in black shirts and heavy jackboots when there is an even heavier load of pasta lurking in the noble Italian small intestine.

More Bedside Urban Voltaire

So, regarding himself as a practical man as well as a poet, does not your man start inventing sundry dishes which will sweep away the canneloni along with the cobwebs of history? The resulting recipes were somewhat exhilerant, or even a little jarring, but they doubtless struck the correct, futuristic, note. Such jaunty little entrees as figpeckers in chocolate sauce, and curried ice cream, were on his suggested carte de menu.

Probably one washed all this down with camel urine, daintily sipped out of a fur-covered cup. However, given such a choice, the Italians naturally continued with their debilitating pasta, and even Il Duce seems to have baulked at the poet's proposed pabulum. He has seen the Future, and it made you sick.

The mad rhymster was, of course, intending to shock, just as Baudelaire was when he vouchsafed that 'the brains of new-born babies had a slight after-taste of nuts', and Baudelaire, being in the nut department himself, knew all about them at that. But nothing that Baudelaire or Marinetti ever said on the subject of scoff was ever as nuts as that which the so-called nouvelle cuisine can currently come up with.

According to a recent report I am out of order in my views on this culinary development. 'Some silly people,' says a Sunday colour comic of a week or so back, 'are saying the nouvelle cuisine is dead.' But this comic concludes that a recent dinner party competition, sponsored by itself, proves that the nouvelle cuisine 'is healthy and thriving in domestic kitchens, where good cooks have assimilated its chief points.'

The chief point seems to be that nobody ever uses Bisto any more and that 'unusual and novel combinations of ingredients are the rule' when it comes to good plain cooking. The unusual and novel ingredients used by the winners of this bizarre competition make Marinetti's chocolate-covered figpeckers look abut as revolutionary as a Sunday morning fry-up. The winners were all designers of some kind, who rejoiced in names like Jeremy or Sara Jane, and who clearly did not live in Airdrie and district where a dinner party simply calls for roast potatoes with the spam.

The judges were 'thrilled' by Richard Cawley's breasts – his chicken breasts, that is – stuffed with preserved fruits and swimming in a puddle of red wine, with the 'lurid dayglo colours of the dish contrasting dramatically with the black dinner plates.' The judges did not reveal what the black platters tasted like.

Black dinner plates were not enough for a fellow contestant. She proffered her skewered mussels and prawns in a mustard bearnaise sauce on a dod of black slate. It would be nice to think that they ate this mess off the slates on the roof actually, possibly during a hailstorm that would show that Marinetti up.

But even our Futurist poet might be throwin', let alone shown up, with the tasty starter of 'papaya and smoked eel with ginger, served in the papaya shell' which another designer designed. If she had laced it with castor oil I wouldn't have been surprised. It is enough to reconcile anybody to school dinners. The description of such repasts as the foregoing is almost enough to get you shoving a finger down your throat.

The nouvelle cuisine was introduced as an antidote to the kind of expense-account grub which shoved everything together as long as it cost half the price of a jet engine. You know the sort of thing – truffles and caviar rolled inside three plover's eggs and then rammed up a pheasant's arse. Expense account cookery is as suave and sophisticated as a sovereign ring, and just as flash. But the nouvelle grub is a marvellous dodge, and all sorts of Trencheryobs are rattling down strawberry and sardine salads with tripe in calamine lotion.

Your urban Voltaire has to make a small confession here by the way. Surprising as it may sound to my readers reeling with the last few weeks' Voltarian sensitivity, I am somewhat of an exponent of that most effete of arts, of cookery. I am, in short, no slouch with a skillet myself. Never am I happier than when I have the Philip Harben stripey apron upon me, and giving a goodly dose of herbs and spices and the wine marinade. If there is a man who can do better supreme of chicken in Marsala and cream sauce with whole garlic, then he is the head bloody chef at Maxims.

But for the gourmets of the nouvelle I will create a special

13

dish; just for them. Marinetti would have been proud of me, for it will describe the fellows right down to the pit of their being. Mince. Presented on a large gravestone. And washed down with the poison of their choice.

Food poisoning
24th August 1984

I don't see how I can be delicate about food poisoning. There is nothing delicate about food-poisoning, except maybe your gastric condition which is positively friable, when you are food-poisoned. So the editors of this blatt are going to have to put up with one of those columns I do from time to time which fall into the 'matters of taste and decorum' file, usually, if it is up to the editors, to remain there and never see the light of day.

Hardened newspapermen have strong non-gastric stomachs when it comes to rape, arson, murder, and massacre, but they go very queasy indeed when you mention what the New Yorker's Harold Ross used to blushingly refer to as 'that bathroom stuff.' That's another thing about a column on food-poisoning. You can't avoid mentioning bathrooms.

When you are poisoned by food you can't avoid bathrooms. You can avoid living rooms, bedrooms, drawing rooms, boxrooms, ballrooms, darkrooms, and breakfast rooms, especially breakfast rooms, but far from missing out bathrooms, you start to live in them. In the week, the last week that is, that food made an attempt on my life I moved everything into the bathroom. At first it was simply the ashtray. By the end of the week I had a library in there, and the telephone, paper, a table, my typewriter. If things had continued I was going to supply an electric kettle and some paper cups.

The first time I knew I'd been poisoned was Saturday morning. I woke knowing instantly that all was not well with the interior Urban V. At first, naturally, I considered a hangover, though I have not undergone such a branding of immaturity for many a long year.

But as I remembered hangovers they were as follows: a dull

thump of a Lambeg drum at the rear of the cerebellum, bile rising in the gorge, a stomach which clearly had nails for its tea the night before, a beating-up by two Plaza bouncers, and a mouth tasting as though you had but recently eaten the entrails of a very old police horse. The Saturday morning in question I felt worse than that, a lot worse.

It was then I considered the idea of alcoholic poisoning. As the pain increased I could almost see my kidneys tearing themselves in two, like a heart of a Valentine card. Goodbye Cruel World, I thought, with some satisfaction. As the pain got worse I came down from such fanciful heights. As the face of the Grim Reaper grew clearer, all the Dylan Thomas style romance began to fade somewhat.

Before the pain and misery got too bad I had even bathed, shaved, put on fresh raiment, boiled an egg. I'd intended making Heraghty's Bar by one o'clock. By the time one o'clock came, then two, then three, the boiled egg was still there, I was shivering into two dressing gowns and a cardigan, and I wasn't sure I was going to make Heraghty's ever again in what was now a short life.

On Saturday I lay like that, fitfully watching TV. There was no point in this activity for the plots of everything escaped me. I was spending more episodes in the bathroom than could be found on the cathode ray tube. That night I dreamt of all the interrupted plots of all the TV shows I had seen throughout the day. I invented feverish endings to them which didn't make any sense and woke up every 10 minutes.

By morning I was mentally exhausted and rather hoped I would get DTs. Even a succession of pink animals would be better than the episodes of Dynasty I was seeing, mini-dramas clearly scripted by Salvador Dali when he'd taken a drop. But Sunday got worse.

By Sunday I had symptoms of typhoid, marsh fever, bubonic plague, and cerebro-spinal meningitis. I knew this because I consulted The Complete Medical Encyclopaedia and Household Doctor, a tome capable of inducing fatality through fright, and which has my father's name inscribed on the flyleaf along with the date, 1936. The medical resources, such as, for instance, leeches, described in this sinister volume may well be out of date; unfortunately the actual diseases were modern enough for me to panic. On Sunday night I re-created The Perils of Pauline. Salvador Dali was still script editor, but was now probably taking draughts of mescalin.

On Monday the doctor came. He was a tall, broad-shouldered, grey-haired, young, handsome fellow who looked like Lee Majors. I want my doctor to look small, slightly Jewish, and maybe with pince nez. I don't entirely trust the ministrations of a hunk of beefcake. Dr. Lee Majors laughed when I vouchsafed my fears about the old kidneys. How was I to know where the kidneys are: I'd always thought they were near the hips. Food-poisoning he said it was and went out laughing still at my ignorance of basic anatomy.

I thought of what I had eaten on the Friday before I had been laid low. I'd had Weetabix in the morning and an expensive charcoal-grilled hamburger at night. I don't think you can get food-poisoning from Weetabix. Maybe the charcoal was off.

The road to recovery is a hard road to travel and I haven't come to the end of it yet. All prospective journeys are planned in advance, and take the availability of public latrines as a major consideration. Nobody else accepts this, of course; damn the sympathy you get. 'Come now,' you can see your chums thinking, 'it's not as bad as all that.'

Trying to explain that the bout of food-poisoning YOU had was practically curare poisoning won't hold up with the sceptical pals. They start to lecture you about pulling yourself together; it's like being read to from a, well, intestinal tract. You almost wish the buggers would get it to see for themselves. And then you think of the misery you've been through in the last week and you know you wouldn't wish food-poisoning on a dog. Not even the dog they made the hamburger out of, the one you got on Friday week, and the one that laid you up.

School meals
February 1988

I once ate a school dinner in France. There you are now: there's not much you can say to that. I have eaten many a school dinner in this land of ours, and, God knows, there is nothing at all to say in that case except maybe that the Scottish school dinner is perhaps a metaphor for our status as an uncivilised country altogether. When I was a little lad it cost you 4/9d a week, and four and threepence if you were the wee brother, and less if you were wee-er than that and nothing at all if your da was idle. Myself, I used the 4/9d on a Friday, (at my shop you had to pay on a Friday), to finance a day's truancy, five Bristol, a game of snooker, and a pie from the Famed Thorn Tree Tea Rooms in Dundas Street. Dear God, I sound like Mollie Weir. The rest of the week I starved.

I did too. My entire adolescence was spent in the throes of hunger pains, and as far as I can see the only things I learned out of it was a ready eye for the juxtaposition of a red and a black and a long term committment to nicotine tar. It was better – the snooker and the five fags – than a school dinner. It still is.

I was not a delicate lad and nor was I the sort of little boy who simply WOULDN'T eat anchovies – I had few fads – but, Goddammit, the school dinner defeated me. They had potatoes which were of a distinctly greenish hue, for heaven's sake. The mince I remember being purple. Both of them tasted of an especially virulent disinfectant. There were puddings which welded your teeth together and which were designed to organise heart attacks. It was as if the Fauvists had been set the task of creating a catering service and had been put on the same working party as the Dada group, overseen by Lucrezia Borgia. I did a lot less damage to myself just learning to smoke the five Bristols.

Another thing about school dinners: the teachers made you eat it. Not only that: there were the dinner ladies to contend with. I will tell you this. Oliver bloody Twist would have behaved himself if he had been faced with a dinner lady.

17

Dinner ladies weren't modelled on the Nazi party: Adolf scoured the world looking for role models and found what he was looking for in the West of Scotland Dinner Lady. There were ones as big and braggartly as Goering; there were dinner ladies with coupons like clenched fists. Dinner Ladies thin and ascetic like Goebbels with lips thinner than the stew they purveyed. Mad Nazi women with the glint of insanity behind their eyeballs and poison in their brains and a ladle to dish it out. If the buggers in the black gowns weren't thrashing you within an inch of your life, boy, there was Mr. Murdstone's sister downstairs in the dinner school giving your intestines a good going-over. Nobody in their right mind gives weans a meal which consists of stewed rhubarb and beetroot. I must be wrong about this surely, but I seem to remember being fed on a diet of the above. Plus lots of the belt. To be young was very heaven. Jesus.

I was a sensitive boy. At primary I went home for dinner. There wasn't very much of a way out of that because my dad was the school jannie in the place I attended. Truth to tell, my dad was marginally worse than the Dinner Ladies but the grub was, I suspect, better. I say, I suspect, because I didn't know what the fodder was like really, but by the reek of it the Dada-ists at my Primary school dinner establishment were at the experimental stage. The Dinner School was lodged in a disused church and there was an air of very old cabbage and ink emanating from it. It smelled somehow of the sort of authoritarianism of the late 'Forties and early 'Fifties. I don't know how to express it really; it was cabbage, rhubarb, old unwashed suits, gaberdine raincoats, spinsters, and smacked bottoms. Now I come to think of it, that wasn't just the dinner school. My whole childhood smelled like that. The Dinner School – that old disused church – that was just the feeling made out of bricks and mortar, and out of the way the adults made all of us live. As I remember it, adults were mostly bastards; the food they gave us was simply another form of corporal punishment.

That the school dinner had been anathema to most
generations of children is undeniable, (though not all children
disliked the grub; I used to feel a sort of contempt for those
boys who liked it and even wanted more), but the truth is that
what the British feed their kids on generally is pretty dire. In
the days of my childhood there was an unenending diet of
stewed beef or lamb, or worst of all, sausages. This was
supplemented by boiled potatoes which had been lying in the
warehouse for a very long time and another vegetable – usually
cabbages or carrots. The high spot of all this was a pudding
drenched in bilious yellow sauce made out of a proprietary
custard powder. At night it was a sticky cake. The school meals
reflected this oddly restrictive menu.

Over the years the working mum syndrome had increased
the amount of pre-packaged and fast food meals meted out in
the average household and today vast numbers of children feed
off fast pasta or pulse preparations heavily laced with soya and
a bewildering number of chemical additives. Meat comes in the
form of burgers and other rissoles. Fish is pre-crumbed. And
potatoes appear only as crisps or chips. Eating is committed in
front of the TV set whenever possible. The school dinner of
today is now reflecting this too.

But let me tell you about the school meal I ate in France. It
was in a school in a little place in Normandy called St. Valery
en Caux. As it happens there are powerful Scottish connections
with St. Valery from both world wars and the 51st Highland
Division (oddly enough for France) became heroes of the locals.
The people of St. Valery are hospitable to Scots and thus it was
that I found myself sharing a meal. It was a very simple meal.
Well, it would be really: it was their version of the school
dinner.

There was a thickened onion soup to start, with bread and
real butter. (This was Normandy after all.) This was followed
by the classic French luncheon dish, potatoes Dauphinois. The
children spooned this ambrosia of potatoes, milk, cream and
garlic out of huge ashets and heaped it on to a plate on to

19

which they piled a green salad. They finished with an apple each. The older children washed this down with wine and water, not cider, as you might expect in that part of France. This was the school dinner, a fairy normal sort of meal I was told.

Of course in France – in the rest of Europe too in fact – we Britons can be easily astonished at the care and concern with which the natives view their scoff. I have seen French dustmen sit down to a lunchtime snack of moules mariniere for instance which would pass muster in the Dorchester or in any of the over-priced restaurants of the U.K. The truth is that the French in particular – and the Italians are not far behind them – are actually educated about their food. The average working class Frenchman and Frenchwoman eats well, more often than not healthily, and last but not least with discrimination. But just ask a French lorry driver across here about what they find in British restaurants. Most of THEM take their own grub with them for heaven's sake. When we talk of the French diner we are talking of an educated eater.

But we know all this: you ALL know this. The British, and perhaps the Scots most of all, are not educated in the matter of the table. In common with most of you I knew damn-all about the possibilities of eating until I was well into my twenties. And it stands to reason that an education of any sort should start early in life. So why not food? And if it can't happen in the home where weans are getting three tons of pot noodles shoved down them and a bottle of fizzy pink rubbish to wash the taste away, why shouldn't an effort be made to do something about food education – and I don't mean learning to cook – in the school. The dinner school in fact.

It seems an obvious place to start. Strathclyde's schools provided a total of 30.3 million meals last year, (of which, incidentally, 18.7 million were given free). It cost over 22 million quid. That is a vast expenditure just to arrive at a nation incapable of enjoying their food unless it is packed with additives and cholesterol. As it happens school meals services all over Britain are changing but not in the way I am suggesting. Instead of the old meat and two veg collopies which acted as the staple in my childhood there will be what is termed cafeteria meals. Like, well, crisps, and chips, and burgers, and lots of fizzy pink rubbish to wash it down. It is said the children prefer this.

Well of course they do. They prefer to stay up all night but no wise parent allows it. They prefer to remain dirty rather than be cleaned. They prefer easy ignorance to hard-fought enlightenment. It is not the job of children to get their own way because they prefer to get it. And it is certainly not the job of an adult to allow them their way on that simple basis. But I am not writing here as a killjoy. I don't want all that junk food replaced by nutritious repasts of what I got shoved in front of me, dishes which always reminded you somehow of washing. I don't even want junk food to disappear entirely either because any nutritionist will tell you that a lot of junk food is perfectly good for you.

I simply find it depressing that so few people get as much enjoyment out of the business of eating as they could. And that the school dinner should continue to be seen as a mere process of stuffing mere pabulum into young stomachs, like fuel in some damned machine. For that old dinner school, with its continued atmosphere of the workhouse, and its 'we eat to live not live to eat' philosophy, leads on to the cheerless staff canteens and the dispiriting meals round television sets. The dinner school can do better, and for that to happen we do not need an educationalist or a nutritionist or some civil servant to organise it. We need a chef. And people who enjoy their grub enough to take kids eating habits seriously.

Lunch   *March 1988*

There is nothing like lunch. It is the only meal worth having really – all the others are what Glaswegian proles call tighteners, meaning a repast designed essentially to sop up the alcohol consumed over the day, or, in the case of breakfast, the night before. Actually the Glaswegian hoi polloi refer to lunch as 'dinner' I am afraid. They are, of course, deeply wrong in this. Dinner is at eight. At night. (I have never understood those mints. Their trademark has a clock with the hands at five past eight. Either their advertising department dines shockingly early or their first course consists of a chocolate sweetie. Either way it sounds dreadfully vulgar).

To call lunch dinner is a positive crime, my dears. Dinner, for a start, is heavy. A heavy word. Suggests Lancashire Hotpot in the dark. Luncheon has the crispness of a morning on it and the freshness. Sunlight and optimism – the beginning of the day and a blue sky in the offing. Lunch is not brash like breakfast, or drear as dinner. Lunch has laxity and luxury. But never lurid. Do not however, sniff at breakfast.

I can recollect a splendid breakfast or two. Once – twenty years ago – about seven in the morning in Edinburgh, just off the London train, I had breakfast in the Caledonian. My brother and me: he is a witness to this. We were tired and weary, at the end of the road and the waitress aged at least seventy – 'I will just get one of the girls' the manager had said – this crone in a black dress and starched pinny came up to us and served us with porridge and eggs and bacon and sausage and black pudding and toast and marmalade and tea and the biggest bloody bill for a meal we had ever seen. It was, after all, Edinburgh. The mist rolled across Princes Street Gardens, I remember, and the castle rose tipsily above it. Both of us were a little drunk from the night before.

When I was a kid, mind, on a Sunday, breakfast was good though, with my Mum doing it and my Da doing us, clipping earholes for being insufficiently open to his socialistic arguments. I don't know: maybe everybody has a notion of breakfast when they were young on a Sunday: a family at war perhaps. Nowadays breakfast is a dismal affair. Muesli and misery. Jesus, people jog for breakfast now.

Dinner I have never properly enjoyed because it gets in the way of going down the pub and meeting people. I have never grasped why anybody would want to spend all night in their OWN house, for Heaven's sake, let alone anybody else's, no matter how good the grub. For a start, if you have lunched adequately there should be no need for pabulum until supper – incidentally another splended time for the ingestion of food. Dinner has got candles on it's table and irridescent talk across it: it is no good unless the conversation is irridescent. You dress for dinner. Women like it: they like dinner. It keeps the men in the house and gives them the chance to martyr themselves doing the washing up while their menfolk embarrass themselves stupid over the Ritz crackers. Dinner is a disaster.

You chaps out there MUST remember how many times over the years that you've been dragged off to some impossible semi-detached maisonette in Lenzie for a stirring night in with a couple you have never met in your life before. The wives are of course pals at work. It is, I assured, worse if your wife is a teacher. And a nightmare if the host couple are BOTH teachers. You have got nothing in common with the opposite hubby and the both of you make the most disgraceful efforts to find a shared interest. There you and he sit wittering about football and neither of you with any interest, or knowledge, of the sport. You sit sipping too large a whisky trying desperately to remember vague snippets you might have casually seen in the back page of the paper. It could and can be worse. You can try politics. You will quickly find out that you are in the house of a raving fascist and will have to keep on saying: 'Up to a point, up to a point' over and over again. When you leave, tired and a little drunk having over-stayed your welcome out of politeness, you hear your wife uttering the dread line. 'We must make this a regular thing', she says. It is no fun at all.

It has to be said here: I am not as one of the unfortunate I have described above. I am not a chap for such an incubus. I am a chap for lunch. The more expensive the better, if somebody else is paying for it. Our own Trencheryob can tell you of all the best places but he likes to travel a hundred and fifty miles to some Highland glen where Julian and Pippa preside o'er gleaming napery and use only local produce right on their own doorstep. Lunch is marvellous. Travelling half the day for it destroys the flavour I should have thought.

No, lunch is when you come off the bustling streets of the city into a little refuge and prepare yourself for hours of food and wine and frivolous arguments for fun with your companion(s). And with a certain knowledge that you are not going to be working at some stage in the afternoon. That you couldn't, even if you were supposed to. There are more working days lost through lunch than there ever are through strikes and I am all for it. What kind of civilisation would it be if its economy would deny lunch? There is, they say, no such thing as a free lunch. Not to worry. I am prepared to pay the price.

Religion

The Kirk
25th May 1984

Back in the old days, when the last word in the spelling book was 'Egypt,' there was always somebody around to tell you that the longest word in the English language was 'Antidisestablishmentarianism.' Later investigation disproves this claim but anyway the word means: being against the notion of being against The Chuch enjoying a few wee bursts of privilege from the State, or even the bloody great swatches of it which they used to have. Naturally I am on the side of disestablishmentarianism because it is not only a shorter word but it also a lot more rational too.

As it happens, the established Church of our own little country is entirely separate from the State and enjoys, indeed the benefit of disestablishment which is why the gorge rises every time some raving idjit writes a letter to the blatts which starts: 'As this is supposed to be a Christian country...' As this supposition is without foundation it follows that the idjit is invariably mistaken in all the following suppositions he will make.

But suppose for a minute that lots of chaps and chapettes are going around thinking that this is indeed a Christian, and not a secular, State and suppose that such fellows got together once a year to discuss their role in the State or whatever, and suppose for a mere second that the media blokes will think it worth while to report what this collection of self-importances utter at their annual jamboree.

Each year we get a week of it all; the General Assembly of The Church of Scotland; held in a big black building at the top of the least augustly named city street in Britain, The Mound. High on this pit-bing, overlooking the shortbread tin that calls itself Edinburgh Castle, the General Assembly meets.

Its boss wears knee breeches and a long black serge coat with many buttons. As no self-respecting human would stick himself into such a dispiriting outfit it stands to reason that

25

this boss is probably the biggest wimp that any boss can be, which is a lot of wimp at that. He will address a large collection of teetotalling miseries, hypocriting knaves, zealotising fools, blundering halfwits who would fail an IQ test let alone any other degree but a divinity one, and also a few decent and extremely frustrated fellows fired with faith.

But each year we get a week of it all; I don't know why. It is doubtless beyond you too that we should have a zillion journalists going off to this shabby little circus and scribbling down the droolings of drivellers in dog-collars, but there you are: we have music critics too.

I have not got much of a good word to say about the dog collars. I recollect at least one sky-pilot who, tired of my gangs' bladder being volleyed into his city-centre manse took a breadknife to it, and a fine Christian act that was too. I remember meenisters speechifying absurdly at prize-givings; I remember their Augustan, and impenetrable, sermons in their churches, and then telling us always to render unto Caesar that which he stole off you in the first place and all the strikers should get back to work.

You might be getting a wee whiff of atheism in your nostrils here: I can't help that. I have never believed a word of what the Christians say: I never understood the words anyway, they were that daft. But I've been baiting Stewart Lamont, himself a back-to-front collar chap, for years, by claiming that I am a convert to Catholic atheism.

Strewth, if I'm going to reject a church, I want one with a bit of style to it. I want a church with great vulgar Italianate paintings on its walls, and stookies with blood and tears upon their alabaster, and kneeling down and mysticism and fancy words like sacerdotal, viaticum, Eucharist, chasuble, diaconal. With absolution and confession and no Trebor Strong Mints and the mothballed disapproval of spinster aunts about it.

And if The One True Church has a gory and shameful history regarding The Inquisition, it doesn't have quite as disgraceful a tradition of telling me that I can't have a drink on a Sunday.

But the Church of Scotland also has a grand tradition of

daftness at Assembly time, a tradition it seems to be holding on to with grim determination. This time around it is overdoing it; not even melodrama, but Grand Guignol. It is sticking up murderers and thieves as men to lead me in the good fight. It is trying to close down harmless wee boozers and them doing more community work than empty churches.

It is putting up with Orangemen and sacking clerics for trying to add a touch of Romish tinsel to their proceedings. It is even trying to get us all to think of God as a lassie. Now we know why catastrophes occur. That's when God nips off for a minute or two to the hairdresser's.

The Church of Scotland, which has a mere quarter of the population as members, and a tenth of them attending with any regularity, and most of them worth a bob or two anyway and filled with Christian charity not to mention contempt for the lower classes, this Church hasn't got a bloody clue.

And despite all the media coverage, and despite their incredible influence in turning my Sunday into a day so bereft of life that you look forward to work, despite all that, just about everybody knows that The Church is utterly, and boringly, irrelevant and so are a lot of the dog-collars up at The Mound this very week.

Do you know what I am doing here, in this week's drivel? There is a word for it; it truly is the longest word in the English language and it was Walter Scott, no less, who used it twice. Floccinaucinihilipilification. It means in 29 well-chosen letters, 'the action of estimating as worthless.' I suspect it was coined for a week such as last, when an Assembly came and went and with nobody the wiser for it.

Following the Band
25th June 1982

Was it not last week that I was woken from my rightful slumbers by the now familiar sound of drums, flutes, and mindless bigotry? Well it was, and the Orangemen commit their celebrations fairly regularly beneath the window of my high-rise pied-à-terre.

Casting a baleful – it was, after all, 8.30 in the morning – eye out of the aforesaid window I saw the usual wee parade of our more history-conscious citizens dressed in their usual tomfoolery. The fat ladies in white hats with the kind of chests which can only be decribed as bosoms. A truly risible sight it is, watching the intelligensia go by. Ach well, they're committed, and so they should be.

The fat ladies were stewarding a wee parade of small girls. There is a certain distaste, is there not, at the sight of children being injected with excessive prejudice. The little girls seemed to enjoy being on show though. I watched them as their wee thin legs stepped along to the sound of the bands. The girls wore kilts of Dress Stewart, you know, that mainly white one. They had white cardigans and white socks and white shoes and a daft wee white handbag each and to cap it all, a wee white beret. Amidst the splash of brightness surrounding them, they looked sort of colourless in all that pale whiteness.

For the boys contrasted strangely with them. The boys were resplendent in bright scarlets and royal blues and plumes and sashes. And while the girls paced along after them, checked all the way by the bosomy matrons, the boys were actually doing things. Their hands were a flurry at their silver flutes, the snare drums were swinging away, and a tow-headed youth was beating the bejasus out of a drum which was too big for him.

For one ludicrous moment it looked as if the drum was playing him, as though he were a German mechanical toy. All of them were doing that wee gallus prancing walk they do. The star of the show was the leader-aff, the boy who has the mace they carry. He threw it high in the air, and twirled it and did a war dance and swung the silver pole around his neck and strutted something rotten. It was pure show biz. And the boys stole the show. For the girls, in their wee washed-out kilts and the white accessories were quiet, demure, and passive as they were chaperoned by big women and they, followed the band. It's what females are supposed to do, isn't it?

Over the years I have had lots of fun out of the Feminist movement. It was easy. Easy to take the mickey out of the

28

deadly earnestness. It was a dawdle to make fun of all those womens's collectives, with all that cropped hair and whining and bleating; the excessive consciousness of being female. Occasionally Feminism became actually nasty as in, for instance, the case of the Yorkshire Ripper, when some inflamed group of wee nebs demanded curfews for men, wild, raping beasts that we were. All of us.

To such women nothing men did was right. In pub or club or anywhere men met on their own we were just groups of pathetic wee boys flexing our machismo. The feminists wanted to be 'allowed' into this exclusive male world, and when they got there they wanted it all to stop. No singing, swearing, bevvying, boasting of sexual prowess – all the rather boorish things which the male species, admittedly rather foolishly, seem to get up to on their own.

Posh fashionable feminists were forever in the women's pages of perfectly respectable newspapers and in their own narcissistic magazines – writing all sorts of junk about The Perfect Man and dresses costing four times your average salary. But then, salaries were never really the point, not even equal ones, for the fashionables. They were all 'top' journalists and ran ad agencies, and had bits of girls in to look after their brats and a Daily to scrub the kitchen floor. The bits of girls and the Dailies didn't have equal pay, except with other slaveys like themselves.

Some of the fashionable feminists had all the savvy and sang froid of Marie Antoinette. One feminist not so long ago wrote: 'I have just the same problems as any man – paying off the mortgage, looking for schools for the children, telling the jobbing gardener to put in the globe artichokes right away...'

But all that is easy. A skoosh. You can get a cheap laugh out of all that damned impertinence, that abject ignorance of the lives or ordinary people. It isn't so easy though when you see wee factory girls shivering away in their nylon overalls and tired out at the end of a shift, and for less money than a man gets. Or seeing wee women hurrying home from work to get their man's tea. Doing all the dishes at the end of every meal. Or when you see women shouted down in an argument or at a union meeting. Or when you see the pressures women are under to conform, to spend their lives underachieving, to spend the first 20 years in pursuit of their very own male, and the remaining years looking after him and his progeny. When you see them simply putting up with all of it.

I am still, I suspect, going to get acres of fun out of the dafter elements of the Women's Movement, but there is no fun at all to be had out of the reality of the harder life we create for the female half of the population. It is no fun for women, having to follow the masters and the boys in the band. Even in, especially, such things as the Orange Order. And the wee girls in their pallid kilts and cardigans shouldn't be following that collection of whooping jubilant idiot boys at all, for it's another banner they should be under.

The real thing
17th April 1987

It is no concern of mine whatsoever what worshippers get up to in their churches. They can act as daft as they like just as long as they don't get to put their beliefs into actual practice and start jihads up against those of us rational enough to damn their fairy stories. But, infidel as I am and proud of it, I'll see you in the hell I don't believe before I allow myself to be called a heathen, or a Philistine either if it comes to that. There are a right few out there who profess religion of one sort or another who are the both.

Oh, sure I am not talking here of such religions as Islam, for instance. Everybody – outside of Muslims that is – can see that Islam is a brutish nasty religion, damaging to all who come into contact with it and a faith belonging to the primitive medieval world. I am not even talking about all those fundamental Christian sects which abound wherever stupidity and a lack of education exists.

For myself they all seem much the same as the other, whether it is prancing about the streets with your head shaved and saffron robes upon you, or dancing about in front of stookies. It is all the same to me: you can do what you like as long as you don't oblige me to follow you into your folly. But there are heathens and Philistines about all the same and among the church-goers too. Some of them write letters to this very blatt.

It has long been a desire on the part of a large number of church-goers to make their religion 'relevant.' I have spent a good few years warning you lot out there of the consequences of the word 'relevant.' Proved right each time I've been. And in the case of organised religion I'll be proved right in that too.

In order to make the theory of church-worship viable the clergy have been hard at work trying to 'bring it into the twentieth century.' Progressive clerics seem to spend more time preaching about 'relevance' and 'the twentieth century' than they ever do about your man Jehovah. One gets a sneaky wee idea that God somehow embarrasses such divines. God was never the boy for progressiveness.

That's why you find the priests getting rid of the old Latin Mass and having you shaking hands with each other and coming out with all sorts of hypocrisy. Back in the old days, I am told, the faith was strong enough that you could get the flock to worship in whatever manner you demanded of them. Now it has to be relevant to the twentieth century. They look not a kick off Proddies to me. The Proddies are worse.

The meenisters of yore are gone. With the exception of the Wee Frees, whose men of God still parade in black homburgs and a theology as hard, black, and as daft, today's meenisters are all the great men for relevance. To this end they hardly don the dog collar at all, and if they do, they sport wee thin soft ones, just like their beliefs, and wear them with trendy sky-blue surplices. They smile a lot and allow a wee innocuous sweary-word across their lips to show that they are not really removed from real life and sip half pints of fizzy lager in public houses. Would that they would confine their modernistic activities to such harmless pursuits.

31

More Bedside Urban Voltaire

I don't know how many of you chaps out there have been in an actual church recently – a Church of Scotland one – but it is a shock to you the first time you hear a cleric at his sermon. Long gone is the beauty of the Bible. The James VI authorised version with all its thee's and thou's has been garaged, probably for ever and the ministers now read from a Bible that sounds as exciting as a message list. I have heard more poetry at a union meeting.

Apparently this is regarded as all to the good because half the nation, well the very wee bit of it who go to church anyway, cannot understand anything but the sort of prose you will get in the EastEnders.

Gone are the days when a dark-gowned minister, the white Geneva bands stark against the black, would intone the glories of sixteenth-century prose to a pious congregation. Gone too is the music. It is all weedy youths playing – incompetently too – wishy-washy acoustic guitars, with songs that are all about Brotherhood and Love and Peace. I wish such chaps would give us peace to be frank with you.

It would appear however that there are readers out there who support these callow songsters and their vapid drivel. A Mr Martin Fair recently wrote to the blatt and made the point that God probably doesn't converse in sixteenth-century English and is doubtless bored with eighteenth-century hymns. It is – to attempt a wee dose of paronomasia – a fair point, but it is hard all the same to imagine God bouncing about the Heavens and talking patter while He listens into his ghetto-blaster.

But the real point about this argument concerning traditional church music as against the anodyne contemporary bilge is this: the old hymns are part of our heritage. Such psalms and hymns as the 23rd Psalm sung to Crimond, or Praise my Soul, the King of Heaven, and many others, are songs which long ago entered the fabric of our culture. Does it always have to be atheists, and beside myself I can think of wee Sir Hugh Roberton of Glasgow Orpheus for a start, who remind the religious of their duties to culture?

I know these airs and wonderful they are too. Some of the

words as well. I have never forgotten the opening verse of the hymn Belmont: By cool Siloam's shady rill/How sweet the lily grows./How sweet the breath, beneath the hill,/of Sharon's dewy rose. Another favourite of my own is The Day Thou gavest, Lord, is ended. But not, I hope, unbeliever as I am, the day of the traditional hymns of the Scottish Kirk.

Oathtaking *February 1986*

Your Urban V here has ever been a leader of men: after all did he not found the Townhead Desert Rats as a little lad. My wee brother was in it and a boy called Strang and his pal Abie Morton. I think they were the only members actually, but anyway I was the undisputed leader. I drew the symbol from an old shoulder flash of my da's. Everybody got a letter of appointment, a badge – worn of course under the lapel and shown at every meeting, well at both of them really – and we all signed a pledge in blood. We didn't really do it in blood: it's surprising how little blood small boys will let you extract and I distinctly remember my brother's refusal to allow what was after all a rather blunt bread knife anywhere near his wrist. We also swore an oath. There is a law against that of course.

Here it is: 'A person is guilty of an offence who administers or causes to be administered, or aids or assists at the administering of,' (it goes on a bit), 'or takes without being compelled, any oath or engagement purporting or intending to bind the person who takes it, to commit any treason or murder'. The Townhead Desert Rats possessed a splended sentence regarding the immediate execution of any member who dared to betray it's existence. The splended sentence for the offence of the law described above, (according to Halsbury's Laws of England 1812, para 838, Volume 2, Criminal Law, and the further 1967 act on illegal oaths), is imprisonment for life, or for any shorter term. I hope to Jesus the law isn't retrospective. I swear I haven't broken the law on oaths since I was ten. But lots of chaps do. Freemasons do.

Freemasons figure largely, of course, within the canons of

British risibility. They roll up their trouser legs and bare their pectorals, and wear silly aprons, and drink themselves into a stupor in their daft clubs. They also take the sort of oath which appeal to ten year old boys. The Townhead Desert Rats were quite in accordance with the Masons: the latter all swear that they will never reveal any part or parts, point or points, of the secrets or mysteries of, or belonging to free and accepted Masons in Masonry. Furthermore the chap with the rolled trouser leg, bare tit, and apron also affirms to the officiating Masons who administer the oath as follows: 'These several points I solemnly swear to observe, without evasion, equivocation, or mental reservation of any kind, under no less a penalty, on the violations of them, than that of having my tongue torn out by the roots'. In the case of the higher 33° division the luckless traitor will get his heart cut out, his bowels burnt, and the top of his head sliced off. I wish I had known all about that lot when I was starting the Townhead Desert Rats – at ten my imagination was lurid enough, but clearly the Masons were even more creative than the young Urban: I could only think of a boring burning at the stake.

It is hard, to imagine all those august lawyers that we know for a fact to be in the Freemasonry running about with their spotty legs to the wind and their shirt tails waving about in it and them solemnly swearing to tear tongues out and slice the tops of heads off. It strikes one too that the same fellows are breaking the laws they are supposed to uphold by even entertaining such absurd ideas. Frankly I'd rather have a chap with the maturity of the Townhead Desert Rats representing me in court, than an elderly idjit who wants to go around slicing chaps up for spitting on the mysteries.

But why get at the Masons alone: there are lots of other daft wee secret societies. If the Freemasonry is essentially non-Catholic, others have their own little clandestine organisations. Leaving Opus Dei out entirely, we have such mobs as the

Mungo Club – widely, erroneously, says the Mungo Club, held to exert an undue influence on Glasgow life, especially on promotion in educational matters, and the Knights of St. Columba. Then there are the Catenians, a group of successful Catholic businessmen who go around doing good works, especially on their own behalf. All the above are said to be organisations of some reckoning at Tammany Hall – I BEG your pardon – at the City Chambers. Of course your Glasgow politician doesn't have to be in any of the organisations mentioned above. It is quite astonishing how many of them are though.

There are usually heavy claims about how much is done for charity, the community, the sanity of the world, and much other drivel, coming from these exclusive little groups. The Rotary clubs are very keen on the above. It has always seemed to me that it should be perfectly possible to donate a few quid every now and again to the less fortunate in the world without having to scoff a damned good dinner with your pals before you do so. I faintly suspect that a certain proportion of the membership of the Rotary mob are in it because it helps their business or their egos. This is cynicism of course, the cheaper the better.

Actually I don't really care that much about whatever effect the Freemasons, or Opus Dei, or the Rotarians have in this country: I suspect it isn't really very much, (though I am bound to get a squillion letters informing me of the sinister influence of Freemasonry on British political and judicial life. The masons are a favourite target for conspiracy theorists). I am sure that Masons aren't the Mafia, though considering the Italian P.9 scandal doubtless our national security network is still excubant. What irritates me about secret clubs is the awful childishness of them. 'Can I be in your gang?' 'Only if you swear an oath and run twice round the playground in your underpants.' It's all daft. Gangs, clubs, cliques. I was in one of them once. The Townhead Desert Rats. I was ten and it didn't last. I suppose I simply grew up.

A thing of beauty . . . ?

There was of course a time when religion in Scotland played a considerable part in the cultural determination. Now, as a largely secular society it is thankfully no longer the case. I, as Dickie Attenborough was wont to say, should cocoa. Not only is Scotland blighted by religion – and by Christianity in particular – so is the rest of the United Kingdom. Christianity is not the worst. The nadir of religions which has any significance in these northen climes is probably Islam, a religion and series of precepts to which I am entitled to an implacable hostility. Mind you, there is just as much daftness in my view about the Jehovah's Witnesses, or the close Brethren, or the boys from Lord Maclay of Clashearn's lodge and talking of lodges the Orange one seems to me to be unnecessarily unpleasant. It is all very well saying that I should extend tolerance on my part to all of the above but as they consistently refuse to show tolerance to my own philosophies, such as they are, and as they insist on inculcating irrationality to their young I am all of an agnostic piece in disapproving of religion entirely. My attitude towards the Roman Catholic Church has always been somewhat benign, partly because so many of my chums are of the Romish persuasion, but mainly because the Jungle Jims have never tried to stop me getting a drink on a Sunday.

It will come as something of a surprise to you lot out there therefore when I tell you that my dismissal of the panoply of churches is a little undermined by my keen interest in matters liturgical. I don't have to agree with the mumbo jumbo of a church service in order to enjoy it. In fact, there is nothing like a spot of the old religious observance to get me waxing poetic. The late Hugh Roberton of the Glasgow Orpheus Choir was a militant atheist but there was never a man who could get more spirituality out of such unspiritual beings as human ones. Roberton could have you joining the ministry with a mere verse of 'All in the April Evening'.

My own background being Calvinistic I am still tied to a

certain emotion when the great Wesleyan hymns come up and it is tears to a glass eye with a score of hymns I know, but the old Scotch, English and Welsh hymns are part and parcel of an entire culture, musical, lyrical, poetical, and political. The lower orders have found culture hard to come by but, by God, they have a great lump of it their in our own heritage. I don't have to believe in a religion with a god to believe in a religion without one.

But there it was on Sunday. Sunday is the day when a minority imposes its demands on the majority and you are wakened in your bed with sentiments expressed by a set of mountebank raving lunatics, soft-headed Oxbridge graduates, and unctuous spiritualists. In short, you are awakened by the radio. And when you come back from the pub and club you are treated to the indignity of Religious TV broadcasts. They are a joke.

Harry Secombe had more logic in the Goon Show than he does with 'Highway', but he is by no means the worst. The worst are wee Scottish lassies with Newton Mearns accents who exhort us all to be excessively cheery in our daily lives because we are getting the Good News round the corner. No they're not. The worst are programmes in which they don't just glorify God, they try to make Him a popular figure and add a touch of populist glamour. It is a very tawdry glamour, even to the mind of an agnostic like myself.

There are guitars and pop groups and everything is endless Fun. The songs are worse than Bernie Taupin can come up and have the unspeakably friendly and beatific grin of the born-again zealot about them. None of the psalms or hymns of the glory days of prebyterianism are allowed at all. If you wanted an especially sickening example of the sort of broadcast which I am talking about you should have seen last Sunday's childrens version of Songs of Praise.

Thousands of innocent little children were crammed into the church. Anybody who knows weans is well aware that the word 'innocent' is a blatant disregard for the reality of brats. The children were constantly provoked into arrant theological nonsense, including every level of multi-cultural drivel as the flabbier sort of Ecumenicist can come up with. But there was one little episode in the course of this farrago which finally turned the Urban V's stomach. A little child stood up and breathlessly spoke. It went like this: 'When I was a child, my speech, feelings, and thinking were those of a child, now I am a man, I have no more use for childish ways. What we see now is like a dim image in a mirror...' It ends with: 'Faith, Hope, and Love; and the greatest of these is Love'.

I know this passage from the Authorised version. The King James runs like this: 'When I was a child, I spake as a child, I understood as a child, but when I became a man, I put away childish things. For now we see through a glass darkly...' This is Corinthians 13. It is a piece of enormous poetic beauty. In the passage the greatest of these is Charity. I hope I can manage enough of it to forgive these religious Philistines who do not know beauty, culture and tradition.

Sport

Celebration with the faithful, and fairweather, Celtic fans
27th April 1988

Anna had been up since early days. Glasses gleaming at the ready. Her daughter Tricia is helping out today. Big John Hastings, the chargehand, has made sure the Guinness is in good order: there's going to be a lot of it rattling down Celtic throats today. It is astonishing how the bar fills up: this is not a trickle of fans, this is an avalanche. By twelve o'clock the bar is awash with over-excited Celtic supporters talking endlessly of football, of goals scored throughout the season. McStay is world-class, Tommy Burns is a dunderheid. I have hardly heard of any of them and care less. By the time that David, the photographer arrives there is hardly space for a pint let alone a camera. But the scene makes great pictures.

This is Heraghty's a small South-side pub with an old fashioned gantry and one of the broadest clienteles surely in Scotland. While there is undeniably a strong presence of Celtic fans there are a number of Rangers supporters who are regulars too. There are even sensible chaps like myself who regard football as something of an opiate. The photographer asks me if I can get the names of the people he's photographing. I know about 80% of the crowd in the bar. There's John Watson in the corner looking elated and anxious at the same time. Bernie the Bolt is getting the boys organised for the bus and whipping up excitement at the same time.

In here I can count at least seven schoolteachers. There are university and college lecturers, several lawyers: I spot two senior TV executives. Last week two MPs were in for the Saturday Celtic love-in. Sadly the Celts did not win the league the week before. They are expected to win it this week. I remember the last occasion their team won this league thing. I saw two 40-year-old men, otherwise sober and sensible, weeping in the bar after the game, their arms entwined. A tall, lissome girl with dark hair and eyes comes in with a big chap I know works in London. So does the girl. In fact she's from London where she works as a stockbroker. Her boyfriend just can't keep away from the pre-match celebrations.

Two o'clock and the bus is about to leave. Outside the children start to arrive for the bus, meeting their dads and uncles just out the pub. Nobody is drunk, except with anticipation. The children are decked out in green and white.

So are numbers of pretty girls. It is the men who seem less inclined to put on the colours. After the bus leaves the pub is emptier and Anna can get around to clearing the bar, for they'll be back by five. I have a word with a chum whom I know to be both a Protestant and a Celtic supporter. He tells me he once had a teacher who spat on his Celtic scarf. It is hard to believe, but it is thus that the old animosities remain.

The first thing to hit me as we parked the car and strolled in to the ground were the peddlars of Celtic memorabilia, scarves, flags, rosettes, and general all round tat. All of them refuse to speak to me, cautious and guarded. Most of them will be drawing dole no doubt: none of them will be paying income tax. Eventually they admit that they make twenty to thirty pounds each Saturday. One of them reveals that he does Rangers lines at Ibrox, too. As it happens the Celtic fans seem less inclined to go in for the regalia than I had seen the previous week at Ibrox park. A small boy was, however, covered in green: he could have passed for one of Robin Hood's Merry Men. He was six, his name was Gary, and he came from Edinburgh. His dad and uncle told me they were from Mayo anyway, but they sounded straight Edinburgh to me.

Inside at the game I discovered that Celtic have already scored. The fans are in full voice. Few of the songs are as triumphalist as the Rangers ones, and are in fact a little querulous. 'For we only know/that there's bound to be a show/ and the Glasgow Celtic will be there.' Later I was to hear the old one about Dublin in the green including the line 'We're off to join the IRA/to the rattle of a Thomson gun.' The Thomson gun is a dead giveaway. The song dates from the Easter Rising.

Folklore more than anything else. Throughout the day I was to encounter very little blatant sectarianism, if at all.

By then, the Celtic crowd seems different from the Rangers fans I had met last week. At Ibrox I have found few middle-class fans, apart from a few bigwigs in the professions. The Celtic crowd went across the entire social spectrum with a large element from teaching and social work I seemed to notice. We are perhaps ten minutes into the game and already the ambulance crews are at work. There is a continuous stream of fans, mainly young, being wheeled off, clutching their ribs or holding crushed feet. It's always like that at big games, says the photographer.

Celtic nearly score and the crowds surge dangerous forward again. In the stand I see George Galloway MP with his kid. For some reason he has his fist clenched aloft. I would have taken George for a Dundee supporter. As it happens Dundee are not coping too well on the park. Off it a lot of the fans aren't too happy either. A well-dressed man touches me on the shoulder and tells me that his season ticket place has been taken by another. He's annoyed but not irate.

This is in marked contrast to the fans outside the ground who are still queuing up. They are hopping mad. This is, of course, the Big Day. This is when all the fairweather fans come out into the sunshine of victory. Small wonder then that the fans who have gone week after week throughout the winter glaur are upset by their failure to get into the ground. Another chum, Big Devlin, limps up to me with a complaint.

'The polis horse has just stood on me,' he says. 'No' that I'm blaming the horse. Can you,' he continues, 'get me in?' In the meantime two young women are making their complaint known to the gentlemen of the press, i.e., me. Both well-spoken and well-dressed, their argument is obvious. The Celtic management should have thought about the potential size of the crowd.

At five-thirty already in Heraghty's the fans are assembled, irritatingly joyous to myself I have to admit, for football seems to me nearly as daft as most other forms of theatre. Already the staff look exhausted. Biff in the corner is brimming over as well as his glass. This is the day they have waited all year for, Biff and Bernie and Wee Frank. I look at young Katrina who seems bemused by the passion of these men, as well she might be. She knows they will be running out of glasses in minutes. In the meantime grown-ups are singing songs and I leave. I do not want to intrude upon their triumph.

Spirited Game *3rd May 1988*

It was surely gloriously apt that last Saturday's Shinty League Final was sponsored by the Weatherseal company, them being a firm that makes double-glazing. Almost all the spectators before, during, and after the match were well double-glazed at that and more. A couple of extra shinty finals in the year and the whisky industry's troubles would be over.

Weatherseal's invitation to the press briefing had claimed that only 'light refreshments' would be served. If the drinks provided at the press pre-match beano were in the category of light refreshment what do they call hard liquor in the Highlands – distilled wood alcohol? I checked the drinks table at the end. The bottles of wine were unopened, not a drop of Martini was missing, and there were nine empty vessels which had once contained Glenmorangie and other such delights.

One of the press chaps, himself a Highlander, had admittedly slurped a gin and tonic but he said this was because he was off the drink. Don't imagine either that the ladies were having Earl Grey tea out of bone china cups; the ladies were rattling down the amber fluid with alacrity. 'Do not drink too much, Dougie,' I heard one huge kilted chap saying to his pal, 'Anyway, I have a wee half bottle for the car'.

An Englishman from the Weatherseal company was wondering by now what manner of game shinty was. He had been told it was a game rather like hockey: now he wondered aloud if it was actually a drinking competition. Well it is, I can testify to that.

In between bevvy sessions though, 24 fit young teuchters go out and hit each other with sticks. Says the Camanachd

Association, the ruling body: 'There is no doubt that no team game anywhere in the world is superior to shinty in the demands it makes on speed, strength, skill, and character.' I suspect a dose of hyperbole here but the last quality is very much in evidence in the playing of the game. It does not really take courage to play shinty: it takes idiocy.

This year's final was between shinty's 'Old Firm': Newtonmore, from the Inverness-shire village of that name and Champions of the North, and the Cocks o' the South, Kyles Athletic, from Tighnabruaich. Nobody could tell me which side was the Proddies and which the Tims but I supported the Tighnabruaich boys because I have chums who hail from there. (The last time I went to that splendid little spot in the Kyles of Bute I went to look for my pal Iain, brother of the shinty legend Russell Thorburn. I recollect going into the Royal Hotel about 10 minutes after morning opening. The bar was filled to bursting with quaffing clients. As I stood with my wee goldie at the bar a middle-aged chap came up to me. 'You'll be a Glasgow man?' he inquired politely. 'Yes,' I told him, 'how did you know that?' The fellow answered instantly. 'Well, you're the only man in here who hasn't got his hand shaking this morning,' he said. Tighnabruaich is that sort of place and more power to it).

They are big lads that play shinty, and very enthusiastic they are too. Enthusiasm is, in shinty, a bit of a euphemism. The purpose of the game seems to be accidentally to disembowel opponents, though you are allowed to score a goal or two meantime.

If rugby is a ruffians' game for gentlemen, shinty is a ruffians' game for, well, not ruffians, but solid working-class chaps. Kyles team were all farmworkers, joiners, building workers, though two of them were drapers, including Andy Irvine, the captain.

Tighnabruaich must be the last place in the world where anybody gets to be called a draper. Kyles also had Barney aged 42. There is an excuse for a boy of 20 to be dicing with death, but at his age I would say Barney would find suicide easier with a bottle of pills.

Newtonmore were all bricklayers and electricians, though they did have a 32-year-old school teacher in their ranks. Some teachers will do anything to get out of the profession. They also had a bloke called Tarzan. He was 40 years of age. He swung that old caman the way his namesake swung through the trees.

'The rules of Play for a Shinty Match' which I read carefully at half time, (I had to read it carefully: by half time I had the double-glazing upon me), state: 'Contrary to popular belief there are clear rules of play in shinty.'

I overheard Iain Anderson, who was commentating from the STV platform and getting bits of his body frozen off in the process, saying technical things which sounded like rules: things about 'By-Hits' and 'Throw-Ups'. The latter I took to be him commentating on the beer tent. Mr. Anderson was clad, incidentally, in a sports jacket of such exotic hue that you could hardly blame the spectators for the odd throw up or two. I know this intrepid commentator is a dramatic chap but this piece of apparel isn't even melodrama: it is positively grand guignol.

It is not the first time though that stars like Mr Anderson have been present on that pitch. Of past dramatic personae there can be numbered none other than the Urban Voltaire, for did I not grace the playing fields myself when I attended the Alma Mater whose grounds these were? Many an afternoon I remember shivering on the wing hoping to Jesus that the ball came nowhere near me, with me in fearful ignorance of the absurd and alien game my school forced upon us all, even wizards of the soccer pitch such as myself.

Dear God it might as well have been shinty, and when I was last there, a quarter of a century ago at least, there was not a drink in sight. And nor was there a bunch of Highlanders about having fun, and making you join in.

Battle of Brussels   *30th May 1985*

I told you so. I told you so last week. It affords no pleasure, no pleasure at all. But it might just answer all those people who told me, absurdly, that I had gone Fascist because I was afraid of the 15-year-old visigoths on the tops of buses on cup final day.

There were those who said I had exaggerated, and those who said it hadn't happened; that 10 minutes on the bus with women and children when the football fans had celebrated their frontal lobotomy operations, had exorcised their dreadful ghosts.

For five days I had every polytechnic lecturer in sociology telling me that it was himself/herself whom I had described and calumnied. They knew it by the description: 'Leather-blousoned sociology lecturer.' It was definitely them they said. The fact that the fellows are all of a piece, that they are even more stereotyped in real life than the subjects of their farragoes of case studies and dissertations seems not to have occurred to them.

Academics are very necessary and I would not have a society which disregarded intellect at any price. We can afford leather-blousoned sociology lecturers. This grossly philistine Government has to be told that and it has to stick.

There were others, too. There were Lefties in the educational psychology business who told me 'frankly,' they said, that I should no longer be in the job, the job of teaching; if I had that attitude. I knocked that back too. The aforesaid child psychologists aren't in my job and I doubt they could do it. If they were in my job all the psychology degrees in the world wouldn't make any difference: they'd turn out as cynical as me or with nervous breakdowns. But I told you so and I have been proved right, oh Jesus I have been proved right.

Wednesday night. Did you know that I commit the weekly drivel on a Wednesday night? Wednesday night I have the weekly drivel ready for typing up and into the subs for them to cut out the bad words and the more abusive passages. I make a hurried excuse to Big Harry and drop down to McEntee's splendid establishment for a small goldie. The drivel this week is a highly libertarian piece about the licensing laws in England. I am right about that too and you will get a chance to read it in the future.

Right now, in front of Desi McEntee's television set I am not

45

sure about Libertarians at all. For what is happening across the little repeating dots of the cathode ray tube would make Liberty look like the Sack of Rome. The Liverpool fans are playing the Juventus ones, or maybe not: certainly the scum of the Earth are playing out the banal evil of their lives. There are, at the moment of writing 34 dead. Play up, play up, and play the game. Where are you now lecturers in sociology that called me Fascist last week; where are you now?

I am watching youngsters fighting first each other, then the Italian fans, then the police, then anybody, then the world. In front of my eyes catching the images on the TV screen I am seeing the sort of violence which we are used to calling gratuitous but which is exactly that . This is a mass celebration of sadism. Armed riot police are being taunted by these British teenagers.

I have seen it all before; strange the Glaswegian who hasn't. Mad Mental Toy, Young Hutchie Are Psycho. We kill Sez Cumbie. This is the nation's youth or at least that portion of it that is excused by some of us because of the unemployment, the single parent, the weak teaching or the heavy authoritarianism of the State.

Youths are throwing missiles at little Belgian blokes, people who speak at least three languages and who have seen too many wars in their homeland and who are not due another invading army at all. On the TV, in the studio, the celebs are talking arrant nonsense, hoping to Christ that the game will go on.

That over-chinned idiot Jimmy Hill is mouthing all sorts of nonsense about the efficacy of National Service, as if getting these kids to paint coal white for two years would make men of them. Let's make them into efficient thugs rather than the anarchic scum which they are at present.

Meanwhile, Terry Venables and Graeme Souness are a bit unsure of the conscription idea. They are both talking Tory all the same. It is hardly surprising considering that they, like Hill, haven't lived in the real world since they were wee lads of

15, and that they earn a right few bob, and that they have the class of education generally fitting to the needs of a Dickensian chimney sweep. If that sounds snobbish, so be it. I can't play football: I don't expect these blokes to make sense of the insensible.

I told you so and not just last week. I told you it years back when the schools started to be all about little children who come unto you and had nothing to do with knowledge, the transmission of culture from one generation to the next, the splendour of ideas and intellect. A grand and pompous statement no doubt. I told you so years back when I said that the kids were not all right, not all right at all. I told you so. There is something wrong and it starts in homes and in schools where promotion rules the roost and colleges and regional councils and I told you so.

Tonight, as I write there are 34 dead and I can hear the typewriters of the sports boys at work. The TV is on and the score is one-nothing. There are 15 minutes to go.

Education

Blackboard jungle
17th March 1984

I got a mention the other week in one of the teacher union journals. Iain Thorburn, an educational journalist of considerable repute and himself married to a teacher, gave me it. It went: 'Jack McLean recently wrote a literate variant of the well-known Sunday Post girn – the kind of stuff for which, a few years back, he would cheerfully have firebombed the Post, or indeed the Herald.' Later still it continued: 'Jack, a classroom teacher and ex-idealist...' The last phrase is right enough. Synonymous. 'Classroom teacher and ex-idealist.' A lot of us feel like ex-teachers as well. You don't call what we do 'teaching' half the time.

But the word which sticks out like a belted hand in the quote above is 'cheerfully'. It is a long time since we had anything to be cheerful about.

A lot of you out there must be getting fed up with talk of teaching. If any of you know teachers you will know that we can't stop rabbiting on about our bloody job. The names of unknown children trip off teacher tongues for two hours and more, on Friday nights in boozers when everybody else relaxes. Munn and Dunning, assessment, discipline... it never seems to stop. For some time now, though, teacher talk is depression talk. Friday nights in boozers are therapy sessions for teachers.

Everybody knows something about schools, though: everybody went through them. Some liked them, some hated everything, some were successful, and some were failures, but everybody remembers school. You remember rows of desks and not being allowed to speak, ink exercises, Technical if you were a boy, Domestic Science if you were a girl, things like Art. There were uniforms and prefects and your older brothers and your sisters, your mum and dad, they all went through school.

Not all of school worked though: you remember that. Most people welcomed the comprehensive and the raising of the

48

school-leaving age, even if it was all done in a pretty half-arsed way. Back then, as educational journalists know, I was a cheerful firebomber, a Progressive, demanding Change for the Future. Well it has changed now. As Iain Thorburn also wrote in his article: 'All the teachers I tend to meet, far from expressing excitement at the prospect of change, discuss their work in terms reminiscent of the chain gang: the lucky ones have got parole, the rest will suffer the daily grind until their release date some 20 years hence.' But please try to understand why this is so, for it is so; bear with me.

Wages: That was the first alienation. The shabby tricks of a shabby management first worked on lowering wages and was to extend to almost every area of working conditions, job security, man management horrors. Truculent employers were matched by truculent union leaderships, often working against, it seemed, their own members. Low wages don't help any worker's morale, and it didn't help ours.

Societal attitudes didn't make it any better. While the majority of people supported, and continue to do so, the teachers, there were others who chipped incessantly away at the educational system. Intellectuals and theorists often made frontal attacks on schools. Listen to this mince from novelist, and at that time 'writer in residence' in a comprehensive school, Angela Carter: 'I think it is marvellous that kids these days have the self-confidence to loll back in their chairs, look a teacher straight in the eye and say: 'Oh God, you're boring.' These extraordinary beings won't take shit from anybody.' This view underlay TV dramas, novels, articles; it became a norm. Pop groups sang 'We don't need no education.' One-dimensional rebellion won't turn into 3D revolution but it'll pay a scriptwriter a right few bob.

Discipline: That got to be a keyword in schools. Once I could hardly utter it, it stuck in my throat like a fascist fishbone. It is a long time since there was much of it in schools. Since the last resort – and if we are to be honest with ourselves in this rigid and authoritarian country of ours – the only sanction, the belt, since that went, the average school, particularly in our cities, has become a bottomless pit of chaos. Nobody knows how far down we can go, least of all the kids.

Schools have become living hells for many teachers, I know this. Young and inexperienced teachers don't stay with it anymore, it gets so bad. In the last two years in my school most of the young teachers left the profession long before the probationary two years were up. Many older teachers set their teeth grimly and apply year after year for early retirement. All of us are used to walking up the road some nights with our intestines tied in knots. More of us take days off with colds and sore throats when once we went in every day, migraines or not. There are a lot more migraines these days.

I know it is hard for many of you to understand, but kids get to you, especially when there are 33 of them in front of you. Kids don't behave like adults, not at all.

When did you last get spat on behind your back, when last were you told gratuitously to 'f— off'? Has anybody thrown an iron belt at the back of your head, or scarred your car in the carpark? They steal cars too. They steal everything, or break it. You learn to lock everything away, but they break in at night anyway and steal and destroy.

It rolls on day after day. Fighting in classroom, corridor, playground. Grafitti everywhere, hitting you in the face 'Tory Toi rool,' 'UDA for ever.' 'Paks out.' Obscenities about teachers, their wives, their daughters. Shaven-headed boys in earrings and national Front tattoos square up to you. 'Ah'm gonny get you, ya bam.' Classroom noise, the constant talking even while you try to teach, the gum-popping: you stand there and plead with them. 'Aw, come ON,' you whine, 'give us a break.' Forbearance and good humour, even the skills you develop over the years, eventually they all crack.

Recently, as the union rep. in my school, I was told of three cases in which teachers had assaulted pupils, just in one week. Not serious cases but circumstances in which the teachers had snapped, eventually and suddenly. The three teachers weren't alone that week. There were five cases of assault actually, for I had committed two of them myself, times when I had taken enough and hauled a boy out unceremoniously and with greater force than I had meant. It is not all like that: it just feels it. And in case you wonder, I have to tell you that my school is not a bad one; there might be better; there are a lot worse.

Into this cauldron of seething discontent – for both teachers and pupils – have come new ways for The Way Ahead. Changes in assessment, in the certification process, in the course contents and syllabi, in the very structure of every level of educational provision in Scotland. Failure to accept the proposed changes, which of course came from those who have not seen foot inside a classroom, if at all, in 15 years and more, failure to express unquestioning enthusiasm for the new proposals has led to official warnings in at least one Glasgow school I know, and will certainly spell an end to promotion prospects, such as exist, for the teacher who cannot display external exultation.

There has even been talk of 'retraining' teachers who cannot 'adapt' i.e. conform. A chilling image it makes: the lines of the non-adapters clutching their thin belongings as they wait for the transport to the re-education camps.

Within the last week (and in many more to come) you will have been assailed with the impending Revolution, with Munn and Dunning, with Action Plans, with new technology, with such drooling fantasies. You will perhaps not be aware that the proposed changes are going ahead without the approval of the teacher unions or of the overwhelming majority of Scottish teachers; indeed few of our educational theorists in the universities and training colleges are convinced by the proposals.

Even if any of us were, the chronic shortage of enough money to purchase such staples as jotters, or to maintain the school buildings in a state of reasonable repair points to the total lack of sufficient funding for even modest forays into new

51

technology. There is not even time on our side. In short, even if the will existed, even were every teacher in the land to work even more nights, even more holidays, very little of the Way Ahead can or will be done.

All of what I have written above will be described by directors of education as 'negative' and – coming from them it is irony itself – 'reactionary.' But I am being positive in being negative: I am telling them and you that the proposals for change in the entire system at one fell swoop are not proposals for real change at all, but merely new emphases in wishful thinking. Some of the changes are shabby exercises in job loss, some are means of covering up youth unemployment. They are not the way ahead: they are signposts to failure and anarchy.

All of the foregoing may sound to you like the Classic Teacher Moan. But there is more to it than that. For a start there are things which can be done to realise genuine improvements in our educational system. I don't simply mean increases in salary, for management platitude and piety has virtually seen that one off. I do mean a change of heart from teachers' employers and a more honourable and realistic approach to employee relations, hand-in-hand with a desire to inject fresh blood into the profession by way of job-security attractions at present not in existence.

As to change for the future: the imposition of impossibly Byzantine and unrealistic processes must cease and consultation, in recent years unknown to those said to be in charge of education, must be placed high on the agenda, and I mean consultation with everybody involved in the school process. A genuine recognition of the value of the working teacher is fundamental to the raising of morale.

A rationalisation of the difficulties in every teacher's actual work must be made. The development of national syllabi which will possess established texts and workbooks etc., and from which each teacher, according to his knowledge of the pupils, can draw and adapt would ease the appalling and duplicating drudgery of creating personal worksheets and texts. The setting up of real and realistic curriculum and assessment committees with the time to operate their expertise within and outside their subject is also required.

As to classroom discipline and pupil behaviour: the schools cannot go on the way they are. Pupil unrest has increased to a point where many, perhaps most, children are educationally affected. And no teacher will be able to last, say 20 years (or less) in the stress-filled schools of today. Every survey, with teachers, parents, even pupils, clearly shows that some form of deterrence to the wrong-doer must exist. Now that the effects of the ill-timed and ill-thought-out abolition of corporal punishment can be seen, surely now there should be a reintroduction of the clear deterrence of the belt.

All the above, and more, can be done: it must be done. There was a time when I would indeed have cheerfully firebombed some of my own suggestions but I know better now. I know that the pedagogic circus tricks and ersatz solutions which are being imposed from above are leading to disaster. For I am not throwing firebombs here as once I might. I am ringing a firebell in the long, dark night.

Give me an 8ft. budgie   *January 1984*

The most risible news story of the new year came, of course, from the United States – from Philadelphia, in fact, where a Professor Ralph Brinster announced that he had found a means of making rabbits, sheep, and dogs twice their normal size.

This mad professor has already created mice several times larger than they are meant to be. Now you know that those 8ft. pink kangaroos you saw prancing round your bed over the new year were really there at that, shipped over specially from Philadelphia. A bit disturbing of course. King Kong grappling with Fay Wray at the top of the Empire State Building is one thing: an 8ft budgie doing the same thing is quite another.

But this little country of ours need not feel too greatly outdone: we have our own mad professors and for a story nearly as daft as the Philadelphia Farrago we need look for farther than in the world of Scottish education. Throughout the last couple of years this has proved a fertile field for looniness but, lads, it gets better all the time and education is beginning to look more and more like a Goon Show script.

Believe me, this blatt's Education Correspondent, the distinguished Mr. John Linklater, has not had a nervous breakdown recently. All he writes is true. I know his reports look like satirical articles for 'Punch,' but then, so do all educational reports, especially the ones the educationalists themselves come up with.

Oddly enough, some of the teachers are in favour of the more recent lunacy: indeed the largest teachers' union, the self-styled 'Educational' Institute of Scotland, seems to be in favour of the impending educational revolution. Mind you, the EIS is a very odd sort of union. Could you imagine the miners' union, for instance, getting their depute general secretary going off to become a boss in the NCB? That's what happened but recently to the teachers' union depute wallah.

It was from this teachers' union that we got the runner-up daft story of the new year. From the union boss himself, a Mr John Pollock, the general secretary, and a man who is presumably going to stay at his post. At a recent Mad Hatter's tea party Mr. Pollock created a master-work of loopiness, that is to say, he composed an open letter to the Secretary of State for Scotland.

Mr. Pollock is claiming, in this letter, that we need an investment of no less than £50m over the next 10 years so that we can 'establish Scotland as a pacesetter in education.' We will need all of this so that the teachers can get a whole year's retraining so that they could find out how to work the many 'microprocessors which are lying unused, or used as toys through lack of in-service provision.' I'll bet the teachers are just giving the weans out books and making them do counting and stuff.

Thae teachers are also all getting too old, says Mr. Pollock, who is, I may say, no chicken himself. Apparently the number of teachers below 30 and 'less in touch with the latest development,' has been halved, yes my dears, halved, in the primary schools and the secondaries are nearly as bad. The idea of all those geriatric dominies hirpling down corridors unable to work a simple microprocessor fills one with despair for the future of our country.

Mind you, the class of idjit we have running our education services are by no means idjit enough to tell you mums and dads out there what they are up to. But the fearless Urban V here will blow the whistle. The Munn and Dunning proposals are couched in a convulated sociologese so arcane that it takes some time before you realise that they consist entirely of making sure that the daft weans don't get too bored, the poor things, and are given Work They Can Do.

As the Work They Can Do is seen by these many educationalists as colouring in everything and playing hi-tech tiddliewinks, it does not take a genius to see that there will be an explosion of private schools, for even the parents of daft weans want their progeny to leave school able to read and write, and that is not creative enough for the educationalists who are in charge of state schools. Labour councillors will deny the above, but then, such fellows are very good at colouring in, it being about all they can do themselves.

The so-called action plan is a move to make class sizes as big as possible thereby releasing expensive teachers for the dole queue and – I'll bet you didn't know this – your teenage sons and daughters will then have to use your money to take buses from the school you chose for them to go to another school three miles away so that they can do Higher German for an hour and rush back to their original school where the German teachers have been paid off and they will use more dosh for the bus and, in fact, it would cost you as much to send them to bloody Eton.

But there is much, much more lunacy than that. Each day some fresh folly finds its way into the schools and into the teachers' pigeonholes. Every day, some new, bright, half-witted idea comes from some promotion-seeking pimp anxious to procure some painted harlot of an educational theory for his under-educated and scarcely elected bosses. Each day sees another parade of pink Emperors round the schools attended by grovelling sycophants wanting the divisional education officer's job.

But the grovelling sycophants will not get the job in the future. I can assure you of that. By the time this educational revolution is over there will be only one candidate for the job. It'll be a rabbit, a sheep, or a dog, four times its normal size, and made in Philadelphia.

Mrs McFadden
10th Jan. 1986

One's heart goes out to Baillie Jean McFadden at this time; it does, it does. Besides being head gauleiter of Glasgow's ruling Labour Group, Baillie McFadden is, it turns out, also a dominie. She is indeed even a bit of a gauleiter in this, because she is a head of her department.

The reason why one sympathises so much with Mrs McFadden is because of the department of which she is the boss. The department, you will have read but the other day, is classics, and Mrs McFadden is both the head of it, and the only teacher in it. Well she isn't really, because there has been another teacher filling in for her while Mrs McFadden attends to important civic matters such as... well I am sure there are important civic matters all the same.

It seems, however, that Mrs McFadden is going to be made redundant, which is really a euphemism for getting the bag, though it is not nearly as chilling a euphemism as the one which Mrs McFadden's employers, whom the lady is said to regard as fine and upstanding, use when handing out the P.45. According to Mrs McFadden's employer, the head gauleiter is 'surplus to requirments.' In short, they do not need Mrs McFadden any more – at least, not as a teacher of classics.

It turns out that it is not only Mrs McFadden who is redundant in the eyes of her fine upstanding employers. It is not only the stand-in teacher who is also presumably 'surplus

56

to requirements' who is redundant either. It is your actual classics which is redundant as well.

This is to be expected. Especially when you consider the reasons that have been given for shoving classics out the door and into the wintry landscape. Lovely reasons they are too, just the ones for our educationists to come up with. Even Mrs McFadden agrees with them. It seems that there is a lack of demand for classics among today's schoolchildren.

Says Baillie McFadden: 'We can't insist that we continue to teach classics. The demand has dropped,' she says, 'there is no doubt about it. Children are opting for other subjects nowadays. It is no longer a requirement for entering various degree courses.' Mrs McFadden sums it up too. 'While adults seem to find classics fascinating,' she says, 'this is not the case with school-children.'

I do not know where to begin with this breathtaking lunacy. I have just had to break off to kick several doors in and smoke eight fags to calm me down.

Let us attempt to begin at the beginning. It seems to my own doubtless eccentric ratiocinative processes that children who start school at all, not only do not opt for any particular subject, but fail in the main to opt for school itself. While it remains true that most of our present Government would prefer children to save money for them by not going to any school, and instead learn a useful trade like picking oakum and the like, it seems to me that the general public want to have brats learning to read and write and know things like that.

I cannot grasp why the children's choice should come into the matter. If you were to give the average brat or bratlet a choice over what they saw fit to study, the Borstals and approved schools would be bursting at the seams. There would be courses in housebreaking and medical merchandising – drug peddling to you that is – for the visigoths with the greatest amount of what educationists invariably call 'working class vitality.'

You can't go around asking weans to study only that which

interests them. If that had been the case when I was a 14-year-old I'd have gone bloody blind in a year and a half. In short, if you want a halfway civilised society – and I presume you lot out there all do – you simply tell the weans what to do. And they do it. And if you want a genuinely civilised society you will tell them to do Latin. And Greek.

As it happens I did neither, I did Techie instead. The result of that is that I cannot hammer in a nail without bending it fast to the wall. My notion of what makes technology tick is that it is all magic. But then, I don't actually care how, for instance, a light switch works, just as long as I am physically not left in the dark.

But I resent my lack of Latin: any writer in that position would. Language is the tool of your trade and mine is blunted more than perhaps it could be because it was not sharpened by the intellectual rigour demanded by a course in Latin.

Of course, it is not only the study of Latin which has been thrown into the cultural ditch which now lies strewn with intellectual disciplines like so many discarded and vandalised supermarket trollies. The decline of language in and out of school has been spectacular. The schools no longer include French and German and Italian, or Spanish, Russian – or even English. The notion that language trains the mind and allows the development of intellect itself, is regarded as almost quaint. What do you need a mind for anyway? The telly will tell you all you need to know, and you can spend the rest of your waking hours playing with your home computer.

The heart goes out to Baillie Jean McFadden, it surely does. She has presided over a Labour Group which saw fit to scrap the old so-called 'academic' approach to education with all that learning and homework and doing what you were telt, while in the meantime the Tories didn't care much anyway and sent their own weans to Hutchie.

The Labour politicians were puffed with pride at their proletarianisation of education, mistaking it for democratisation. There are two words of classical origin, in this case Greek, in the above sentence. Here is another one, just for Mrs McFadden. Hubris.

Teacher's New Year
26th June 1987

I started this: Liberation Day. The Teachers' New Year. It is nothing to be proud of. Time was when the dominies of our land went for a celebratory cup of Typhoo and a Co-operative fern cake; a pink meringue if you got in early. It is changed days now. Was it not the other day that I overhead two building workers in conversation? You used to call them navvies. You used to call teachers Sir. The two construction industrial boys were organising a date for their next meeting, which incidentaly fell on this very day. My eariewigging of the conversation bore sufficient fruit. It transpired that two lads would not be meeting at any of their normal haunts of this Friday night. Their normal haunts, they said, 'would be hoatching with thae teachers'. It might be seen as some kind of indictment. I invented some of it.

I invented the phrase: The Teachers' New Year. The entire process has becme an institution. We will be doing the coal and the Black Bun next. What I can tell you is that when I first started in the domimie business a couple of end-of-term halfs seemed in order but a lot of water – not to mention whisky – has flowed past that fabled bridge ever since. Today the Teachers' New Year has become part of the social calender of the underclass. A drunk and vomitting pedagogue is excused on this night of nights. I write this every year. It is called my End of Term Report.

Some headmasters don't like it: every year. They crack under the strain of their idealism and complain that thae teachers are a fine bunch of Harris Tweed clad wimps who should not be maligned by reality. Educational officers who last stood in front of a class in the dark days of reaction and literacy get shockingly upset. I have gone for the above, right for the throat, for years. Sometimes I went for the councillors too: it was a skoosh.

It is not as easy this time. For a start I have joined the councillors: I have even been able to hobnob with them. As the teachers' representative on the Regional Council I have discovered that the Council folk may be simple country folk but they are not all daft. That the Officials are not daft at all. That, despite a long and bitter industrial action campaign, most – or anyway enough – teachers are practically halfwits.

It is simply not possible to explain to anybody why or how the dominies voted against an unsatisfactory report into their wages and conditions and voted for the same thing, only worse, less than a month later: especially as they voted massively against the first offer, and at the same percentage, *for* the second one. As a Union activist you feel that stupid. Nobody could ever deny that the retiring General Secretary of the main teaching union, the E.I.S., is a very smart man. Nobody could deny that he has been seen, at the end of the day, as not very smart at all. I don't know anymore, right or wrong. There is, after all, posterity to judge.

Last year I was threatening the employers, from councils to Education Secretarys in my end of term report. The year before I was saying that the dominies were off their knees. This year the teachers couldn't threaten bloody diarrhoea. But the bosses and the promotion seekers and the rest of the campaign to destroy Universal Rationality could and the development of what such fellows call 'Progress' would make Crimean dysentery look like constipation.

You readers out there don't know what's in store for your brats. You are going to have a thing called T.V.E.I. shoved in front of your progeny. The acronym stands for the Technical, Vocational, Education Initiative, and it means that we have found a modern-day equivalent for sticking bits of boys up chimneys. Lots of dominies think this is good because it will give them more money to spend on drivel and also the chance for promotion so sod off anyway. Not to worry, after two and a half years industrial action in which the educational system may well have entirely foundered in a cultural disaster, lots of teachers would have licked out the school lavs for an extra fiver. I sound bitter.

Oh, there is lots more on the agenda. They will be closing

schools. That'll have you parents in a fearful bate. They will be giving young teachers the bag: I am sorry, they will 'not be renewing their contracts'. There will be lots of teachers 'surplus to requirements'. The teaching unions will be impotent and no wonder because they proved that during the last campaign. There will be lots and lots of utter mince.

The Ethnic Minorities Project will go from strength to strength and in the process be able to develop a level of racial tension hitherto unknown, or anyway, resistable, in this country and as a result there will be lots of jobs for blacked-up racist anti-racists, (I will get stick for that). There will be things called Standard Grade and Foundation Science and Assessment Procedures involving Grade Related Criteria. I know: I don't understand any of that any more than you do. I know this.

The teachers went out on strike for more than money, three years ago. They went back, at the end of the day for just that. Scottish education is worse than it was before that tragic dispute and it is not going to get better. None of the proposed changes – *which are going to occur* – will happen in the fee-paying and the private schools. This is my end of term report; the one I do every year.

I wish I had better news for you, but I don't. It is the Teachers' New Year though. Go out and multiply. And join us for a drink. A tear in a glass. Aye.

And now I am out
October 1987

I can only think of the names of two of them. One was named Rowan. He had a face like a brain-damaged angel. The other was Brannan. He was small, shilpit, with features somehow inchoate, like a snotter on a pavement. There were others too but I can't recollect their names as easily. I don't want to; in fact I want to forget the names of the last two. In a few years time I will doubtless encounter them and their classmates in some pub or other. I will tell you this: when I do they are going to get a boot up the slate, the scum that they were. They were all in the third year class that I took, the last year I was in teaching. Don't even think about telling me they were only little boys. We are not dealing with boyish mischief here. It isn't the William books. They were bastards. And they put me out of teaching.

I had seen similar phenomena over the years with colleagues. There had been a few occasions when as an Educational Institute of Scotland representative – a kind of shop steward – I had been forced to look after the interests of teachers who could no longer cope, who had been got at too long, who had been broken on the wheel. I may say that almost every time I had witnessed this I had noted a salient factor was that the rest of the staff, right up to the Head teacher and his chums, had long lost the notion of support for their suffering colleague. Now it was my turn.

I was sort of due it, after all. A prominent journalist for some fourteen years, widely if erroneously imagined to be 'earning a fortune', (ALL teachers fondly suspect everybody else of earning more for less work), a thorn in the side of the educational establishment often urged on in that endeavour by colleagues anxious to upset their employers without being seen to do it themselves: I was ideal. My colleagues threw me to the wolves. In this case the wolf was the sort of dumped class which is always given to the Art teacher. When my former colleagues gave me a rather handsome presentation, the new principal teacher made an equivocal speech and a colleague of eleven years for whom I had done many a favour refused to turn up because she felt I was some kind of flyboy. God rot them. At the end of the day I had scarcely more respect for teachers than I had for the weans I had been teaching for the last few years. And I had contempt for most of them because I had seen too many of them grow up to be graduates at the BAR L and other such colleges. Most of the girls were up the stick within months of leaving school. A large number of their children will be taken into care within the next few years. There's another thing I don't want you telling me: about how I should have respect for other human beings. I lost that brand of sentimentality a long time back.

But it wasn't always like that and neither was I. I started back in 1968 in a junior Secondary School in Lanarkshire and it was a wonderful job. It was the best job in the world, teaching children Art. Over many years that experience sustained me, especially when I encountered, increasingly rarely, pleasant hard-working, NORMAL children, with normal mischief and normal attitudes of some kind of respect, even liking, for me. But then I loved the work so much I decided to become a teacher for life.

But things changed dramatically in the early 'seventies. There was the Raising of School Leaving Age for a start. This was, as every single educational initiative has been since, underfunded and ill-thought out. There was the business of turning the old Junior and Senior Secondary system into Comprehensives. There was a national disaster called Regionalisation by which a massive proliferation of careerist administrative and executive posts with sod all to do in them but think up drivel well away from the classroom, was created.

Worst of all there was an upsurge in a kind of unctuous concern for the Whole Child. For a spell I was under a spell myself: I too was a Progressive; as full of liberal nonsense as it is possible to be. To my shame and regret I unleashed my own self-indulgent bile on to a Scottish education establishment which had become so old and decrepit that it viewed the progressive attack through pince nez and then retired. It is only in the past few years that I have come to understand the astonishing achievements of such figures as H. Stewart Mackintosh and John S. McEwen, respective directors of education for Glasgow and Lanarkshire. Later I was to discover that the Scottish Office did not share the otherwise universal respect for these men who had done so much. By the 'seventies the Scottish Office, the Scottish Labour politicos, ever anxious to destroy the excellence of a system in which many of them did not shine themselves, the careerists in teaching, many of them academically less fit than their

63

predecessors and keen to put the boot in, and the sort of sub-Marxian liberal which indeed I may have myself – by the 'seventies the whole crew were poised to undermine the entire, much valued, Scottish educational system of which the nation had been so overweening in its pride.

It was an easy process. You simple questioned everything which had gone on before. You undermined it first and then you said it was anachronistic and then you let the old buffers shuffle off the stage and then you promoted every self-seeking little crawler you encountered and then... and then you substituted as hare-brained an idea as you could come up with and justified it by telling everybody, but especially the labour politicos, that this meant An End To Elitism.

It certainly did too. Good schools with long traditions were closed overnight because too many middle-class kids were benefitting by their existence. (The middle classes simply went on sending their brats to better schools and organised grants and tax dodges). The 'difficult' subjects like Latin and Greek went early – they weren't 'relevant' to working class children. Soon every subject was tampered with on the basis that we were dealing with some so-called average child and the notion of such a mean was lowered yearly. Eventually it was decided to castrate the curriculum entirely and Dr. James Munn, headmaster of Cathkin High School, and a sophisticated, well-meaning and intelligent man, chaired a committee to look into the dismantlement of the Scottish educational tradition.

It took some years to produce the report and it was never implemented really, egalitarian as it was in essence. It emerged eventually as the Standard Grade, the final nail in the coffin. The Standard Grade farrago possibly heralds the end of universal education itself, let alone the pursuits of excellence, and I am not sure that the Tories are entirely unhappy at the poverty of educational provision which this development represents for working-class children. It doesn't matter what the Labour Party think of it. Even before Premier

James Callaghan's near-illiterate Great Debate speech, and before too, the Labour Party has encumbered education with an ideological goal of equality impossible to create or administer, and almost sinister in its lack of intelligence and logic.

Meanwhile other social forces were at work. The authority of the classroom teacher was taken away firstly by banning corporal punishment and then by establishing such rights to the visigoths and their parents as would ensure that classrooms in many schools would be chaotic to the point of anarchy. Spurious ideas, fuelled by yet another career lobby, of multi-culturalism, (in fact a process of denigration for Western European civilisation), fired the school curriculum. More work was ladled on to the shoulders of the teachers weekly to the point at which they began to strike every five years just for respite. The last one lasted two years and its disastrous effects have yet to fully emerge. The EIS general secretary the redoubtable John Pollock, who had tried to hold some kind of sensible consensus, was at all times constrained by the fact that he had a collection of raving Trots in Glasgow, some of whom had the right idea, and a swarm of Highland conservatives, few of whom had any ideas at all, and thousands of other teachers who would lick the toilet floor clean for an extra fiver and Principals with none at all.

Twenty years after I had started as a teacher I no longer knew what I was supposed to be doing, disagreed with everything and had classes of weans who told me to fuck off at will, threw crayons all over the place, and stole and vandalised at night. There is no school in any urban area which isn't in a condition that would close an average factory down as a health hazard.

But the most dispiriting thing for me is that I keep on encountering teachers who pretend not to see this reality, whose eyes are dimmed by the flitter of a future career or who inist on a sentimentality about children, schools, culture itself, and who are outraged at any picture of the unvarnished truth.

More Bedside Urban Voltaire

I also encounter social workers with the same attitude. The two named above are the worst but such beliefs course through the whole of the middle class philosophy about perception of schooling. The lumpen proletariat don't care what happens in schools but don't mind they snobby teachers getting their noses rubbed in the dirt and the upper classes don't send their kids to state schools anyway. The anxiety of the respectable working class can easily be coped with.

It isn't much of my concern now, I suppose, but the sense of rage is still there. The sense of actual rage that all the people I have castigated above, all the people who created this cultural calamity over the last twenty years and continue to sustain it, are as secure as fascists in their beliefs that only they are right, and everybody else is wrong. Twenty years ago it was that I believed in education. But back then we had a different reality from the nightmare of today. Now there are people who tell me I should never have been in teaching and I am inclined to agree with them. And now I am out.

Things

Favourites 28th Dec. 1984

Here is some drivel:

'Girls in white dresses with blue satin sashes,
  Snowflakes which fall on my nose and eyelashes,
  Brown paper packages all tied up with string,
  These are a few of my favourite things.'

I can hardly bear to reveal to you some of the further samples of this particular songstress's favourite things. They are of the class of cloying sentimentality which one would expect from Miss Julie Andrews, that Great British Warbler whose screen persona is that of the world's most famous virgin outside of Marianist theology. I am beginning to wander here, lads. We will start it again.

I simply refuse to upset you at this time in the morning with the remainder of this appalling lyric. Those of you with the sort of wives who cry at Bette Davis movies instead of laughing hysterically; indeed those of you who are the sort of wife, will doubtless already know all of the words anyway. I will leave you alone at breakfast and give songs from 'The Sound of Music' a miss: it is hard enough to keep muesli down at the best of times without getting the old oil about snowflakes which fall on your nose and eyelashes.

Favourite things? Dear God, only a woman could think that one up. A woman with progeny at that. Great milky things, soft and saccharine, sticky and sentimental; that's your average young mum. I take a hard line on mums. Should be shoved off to some large tribal hut, they should, until the little ones are old enough to stop bothering civilised society and matronliness has burnt itself out.

Favourite things? *The Sound of Music?* Brown paper packages tied up with string? Grumpy the seventh dwarf had a word for such nonsense. 'Mush' he called it and mush it is: mushy and slushy and cute and cloying as a chunk of Turkish Delight, as pink as a placenta. I'll show you chaps what unpleasantness looks like.

More Bedside Urban Voltaire

Having such things as favourite things belongs to those who have identified the limitations of their life, and glad to do so. It is like being able to say what your favourite film or food is. It must be obvious to the rational human that any fellow who can blithely inform the world that his favourite book is... is practically illiterate and reads with his finger pointing at the words.

It is almost impossible to get away with any prattle about favourite things without it sounding like prattle. Even Scott Fitzgerald couldn't do it because he wrote the following: 'I liked doctors and girl children up to the age of 13 and well brought up boy children from about eight-years old on. I could have peace and happiness with these few categories of people.'

Old Scott did his fair share of prattling as the passage went on. But look how much better it would have been if he had held the above in contempt. I mean, he could have turned it into a thing of delight in which he expressed his loathing for physicians because of their air of smug omniscience, their air of simply humouring the lunatic; for the fact that so many quacks smell of nicotine, or of mothballs, or, in the case of one I know, of moths.

Fitzgerald could have detested girl children because of their inability to keep still, constantly skipping about on pavements like some damned demented dervish, or because of their apparent beliefs in sheer potency of hair ribbons. As for well-brought up boy children over the age of eight: there are no well-brought up boy children of any age whatsoever. The only way you can well-bring up boy children is to chain them up all day. You know it yourself: it is a lot more fun to dislike things than it is to favour them with your regard.

In the context of the above it must be clear to those readers who are always telling me that I have too many likes and dislikes that, in fact, I have hardly any likes at all, and one of them is disliking things.

By now, Dear Reader, you should know well my dislikes. Computers, jogging, hard-line feminists, television, BMX bikes, wine bars, Conservatives with a large C, anoraks, people who speak for minutes with their eyes closed: each of the above demanding withering contempt. Also amusement arcades, the TV column in the Sunday Mail, progressive educational theorists, barmen who put ice into your whisky without asking if you want it, so-called traditional folk music, all the STV presenters except Bryce Curdy, and vegetarianism. There is a list to be going on with. It is a dawdle just setting them down in print.

But presenting you with the favourite things: that is a harder task. There are colons of course; the semi-colon too is a decent little fellow. I am not merely talking of obvious little favourites like sex or whisky, but of the class of item or phenomena which makes life worth living besides making love or rattling wee goldies past the thorax.

Things like old films and ginger snaps, real coffee, cuff-links, good restaurants with wood-panelled walls, the sight of a pretty woman in pretty clothes, bright neckties, cheery shop assistants, a book you keep reading till dawn breaks, dawn breaking and frosty mornings, Elvis Presley, Radio 4, winning at poker, and all the colours except puce. That is the stuff to give the troops.

You see what I mean about prattle the moment you start drooling about favourite things. The next thing you know I'll be salivating about bright copper kettles and warm woolly mittens, not to mention raindrops on roses and whiskers on kittens, and if I ever get to that I shall be all washed up and ready to be led gently away.

At odds with this bright vision of the future

6th Sept. 1989

'I note, Evelyn,' I said to the lovely chatelaine of the grandly named Elcho lounge bar, 'that some crowd of religiosities have for once got it right.' Smartly avoiding buying another round for Benny and his pals, I continued: 'The Exclusive Brethren,' I said. 'Another collection of bananas. Got it right though. Were more to be like them,' I slurred, 'the world would be a better place and children get to be taught proper and the like.' The Exclusive Brethren are currently demanding that their brats be exempt from compulsory teaching about computers. I hate computers.

This band of religious maniacs have decided that computers are evil, a conclusion to which I myself have come. The Brethren say that these wicked machines are so because of what Revelations 13, verse 13 had to say about them. Frankly all those thirteens look a bit sinister at that. Not nearly as sinister though as what Revelations 13, verse 13 had to tell us.

'It works great signs, even making fire come down from Heaven to earth in the sight of men,' saith this splendid passage. 'It' is one of these beasts that Revelations goes in for and has two horns like a lamb and speaks like a dragon apparently. Sounds just like a brat to me, even a Brethren one. I am at a loss as to what the merry men of this sect are on about really, but I am sure they have a point.

Actually what these people are trying to say is that computers are a scientific imitation which rivals what God has put into living persons, making man independent of God and leading to infidelity. Well, the lads have a point at that. They have just not gone far enough.

The truth is that computers do not think and neither do the weans anymore. Computers do not give you ideas and the weans subsequently don't have any. What the weans (and virtually every adult under the age of 33 as well) have in place of ideas is notions, like what expectant mothers are said to have.

Those who promote these ghastly devices and its ghastlier jargon have the notion that children should be what they call 'computer-literate'. In reality this means that children should play with their fingers and make designs on silly screens. They would be better employed breaking stones or cutting flax or whatever workhouse brats were made to do back in Victorian days.

Computers are to thinking what Bugs Bunny is to Moses.

The promised land that Bugs Bunny will lead you to is a land of uncompromising idiocy. It is a land in which every little whim is met and you spend all day lying on rubber lilos in swimming pools in concrete hotels in Corfu getting injected with a slurry of Coca Cola and bacon-flavoured crisps while peasants in other lands break stones and cut flax and so on. This is the world of the future. I am getting middle-aged.

I am, too. I don't understand anything anymore. I don't much like anything anymore either and spend my days wandering about looking for places and things and people which and who seem normal, before the aliens came. Everything is so damned bright nowadays. You get your eyes seared with luminescence as well as your ears blasted off with the lurid diapason of the discotheque. Have you, for instance, seen 'Smarties' recently?

Remember the days when gentle aunts brought you a tube of these delicious chocolate beans? I was an aesthetic little lad myself. I loved the subtle hues of these sweetmeats; the pale browns against the dark browns, the lilacs and pinks the colour of sweet peas, the sudden drama of the cochineal scarlet, the gay radiance of the orange and the lemon. Those tones are too subtle for today's world.

They have introduced a blue of a shade virulent enough to delight every idjit who ever watched his TV set with the colour full up. This is what the weans and the world wants. Verve, vigour, vim, especially vim. Scouring powder for the brain, erasing everything on it.

Computers are part of this bright, retina-shattering vision of the future. Oddly enough they have become somehow the objects of worship and idolatry too. Millions of half-witted mums and dads have got it into their heads that their children will never come to anything unless they can play games on their home computers; forget all that reading books. 'You can do all that reading in your spare time' they will doubtless be saying to their progeny, while force-feeding them with Lurex pot noodles. That's what I said to Evelyn the other day anyway. She didn't seem too impressed at that.

Domestic minutiae *April 1987*

I don't know why daily life defeats you: it just does. Some of the daftest people in the world are impervious to this precept. Just take a look at car-drivers for instance. There are chaps with the brains of rats who have learned to drive. I am feared of a dodgem at the shows, and I have an I.Q. of a Steve Davis snooker break. I can't do anything. It is the brains. When you see me holding on to my cranium in Heraghty's Bar it is not the drink in me: it is the sheer weight of the grey cells. Grey cells or not, I am practically halfwitted when it comes to the most mundane of domestic tasks.

Some English bint wrote but recently in a New Technology blatt: said she intended to be different from every other columnist in the history of English Literature. Said she would not be writing on the 'minutiae of domestic life'. The bint will last a month, if that. Columnists never write anything important because the things that columnists find important are rivetting little items such as the meter-reader, the shocking cost of German lager, why ballpoint pens burst in the breast-pocket of only light-coloured suits. Columnists – unless they are unreadable – find nothing of any interest whatsoever in the present conflict in Beirut for instance. As a breed we columnists are pretty sure that conflicts in Beirut are going to go on forever and generally allow public outrage to go the way it always does which is to say into the ocean of apathy. Domestic minutiae is always with us and proves a right little earner over the years for hacks like myself.

Domestic minutiae is a fancy way of saying that you are always going to need a clean shirt or that sooner or later you are destined to require binliners. It is different for your Urban Voltaire here to admit such needs – we intellectuals would rather indulge in a spot of speed-reading of Spinoza and the like – but admit it I must. I am regularly accosted by readers who spy me in the fishmongers and gaze in wonderment at the sight of Scotland's greatest literary figure with a poly bag filled with soap powder and other such minutiae of domestic life. I said I was useless at such tasks. I am worse than useless.

Take toilet paper. I almost always forget to buy toilet paper. I end up using Kleenex tissues. Sometimes I end up using this very blatt. Even when I do remember toilet paper I invariably buy what I think is toilet paper but which turns out to be kitchen roll. On one glorious occasion I found, to my discomfort incidentally, that I had purchased a roll of aluminium foil. Even such a hardy chap as myself balked at that.

Simple things which simple people, such as women for example, take for granted – Hoovering comes to mind – prove my undoing. I have got the only Hoover in the world which blows instead of sucks. I read the instructions not so long ago about de-frosting the fridge. Robert Falcon bloody Scott could not have coped with the amount of ice in my fridge. Jacques bloody Cousteau would have ran out of oxygen had he encountered the positive SEA, my dears, which ensued when I 'followed the instructions' in the refridgerator pamphlet. I can't do anything right. You should see me at the ironing board.

Was it not just the other week that I decided on a quick ironing session? Normally I iron a shirt immediately prior to going out of a morning. The front, the cuffs, and the collar. Why muck about? But your man here is a stickler for rectitude. A wee dose of starch in the collar is necessary. A little stiffening in the soul it is. And the other week there I ironed four shirts. Lightly starched collars. One has, after all, to put on a bit of a show for one's public.

Oddly enough, there was something wrong with the can of spray starch. It was sort of lathery; a bit too frothy somehow. Didn't iron too well either. I looked at the collars. They were sort of, well, melting. I looked at the can of starch. It was not, and by no means, a can of starch at all. It was, in fact, oven cleaner. From now on I am going to buy this brand of oven-cleaner. From the way it attacked my shirt collars I reckon it would clean up a processor in Chernobyl.

I am not very good with cans incidentally. I still remember spraying under-arm deodorant in some haste in the morning only to discover that it was shaving foam. I am worse with can-openers. I have got permanent scars from can openers. I don't know if Jimmy Boyle, back in the old days, ever considered a can-opener. I can commend the buggers for fatality. I told you. I can't do anything. I don't intend to in the future either: I am going to leave the minutiae of domestic life to lesser mortals in the future. I have a notion of a French maid, saucy as you like, in a short dress and petticoats. A suspender belt and nylons would be nice.

Fear of things
July 1985

In my youth about the only emotion a male could admit to was anger. Showed the fierceness of a warrior, it did. Of course, in recent years the womenfolk have tried to change the male out of all recognition and as a result we have thousands of home-based wimps in stripey aprons cooking Sunday lunch, and parenting like idjits. This bunch of milksops make no bones about tenderness these days. Instead of administering a quick clip round the wife's ear, they now sit down in a concerned and conscientious way and 'talk it through'. As most women are perfectly aware that this is damn-all but another strategy for the bugger to get his own way it makes more than sense that some wives have taken to rattling the old saucepan around her tender mate's tender bloody ear and quite right too. Anyway, even hardened feminists don't want tearful wee poofters as husbands. I recollect our own Julie Davidson admitting, in a non-plussed way, that she fancied Rhett Butler in *Gone with the Wind* something rotten. As I remember, Julie confessed a distinct preference for Mr Gable over the soaking wet Leslie Howard. The truth is that tenderness, except perhaps in private and in bed, is not a becoming emotion in a man. But the very least attractive emotion must be Fear.

Fed as I was in childhood on old Edwardian *Chatterbox* annuals I responded mightily to that age's calls for courage. I admired such chaps as the young Nelson. ('Father,' the little lad is reputed to have asked his papa, 'What is Fear?') There was not a trace of fear in any decent boys stories. R.M. Ballantyne took courage for granted. Real life stories were about such manly little fellows as Jack Cornwall, the youngest-ever V.C., and courage made a man of you while cowardice branded you for life. Reading *Lord Jim* as a teenager I utterly despised that eponymous protagonist.

Sure, I had a decent supply of physical courage myself. Always the stoic I was. Even the frequent beltings at school I met with the greatest philosophical detachment I could muster, at least on the outside. I recollect a teacher once doling out six of the belt to me, finishing off by asking me if I had had enough. Your Urban Voltaire, now the champion of dominies everywhere, answered promptly. 'No Sir,' I remember blithely replying, to the delight of my classmates, 'I could manage some more'. The hands were dropping off me at this point but I would, then as now, hang myself for a good phrase. Not to be outdone by a bon mot, my assailant stated that I was obviously 'thirsting for blood', and delivered three more strokes before being stopped by a passing teacher, now a distinguished University professor. I was sent to the lavatory to wash my hands for some inexplicable reason. Washing my hands did nothing at all to assuage either the pain or the shock. There were indeed, in the past, teachers who gave violence a bad name.

Violence has afforded few slights on my physical courage. As boy and man I have avoided fisticuffs and boozer battles, but not to the exclusion of personal pride. In truth I have always been of a somewhat pugnacious temperament, and despite a sensible reluctance to expose myself to danger have been throwing the odd punch or two since I was old enough to put my dukes up. At fat and forty though I would prefer the knuckle sandwich to be off the menu of Life for good. Fat and forty I am, and fearful.

For Fear is always with us in some guise or other. I am a bugger for the irrational ones. It is irrational, but somehow acceptable, that one should be scared of heights. And I am

75

scared of heights. There is, of course, no rationality at all in finding myself rigid with blue funk halfway up the Scott Monument in Edinburgh, or the Wallace one in Stirling, or the Georges Pompidou Centre in Paris. But in all three places I have found myself unable to move, up or down, dizzy and near to vomiting, while small girls scamper unconcernedly up the stairs.

But in the case of such a vertiginous response to high places I can only claim in my defence that ah cannae help it. The physiology has taken over from the psychology. (Though it has to be said that my fear of heights seems to lie in the desire I have to jump out of the open windows or off the top of the mountain: if that's not psychological I don't know what is).

But how do I explain my utterly illogical fear of insects. I can just about manage to overcome this with the common fly, though I am not too happy about any creature which lands on your steak, vomits and stamps that in with its feet to soften up the meat, devours it, and excretes at the same time. I can at least bring myself to brush flies away. A moth in the bedroom though is enough to have me kipping on the sofa for the night. I hate their fat ugly grey bodies; I hate them bumping into you. I loathe all kinds of creepy crawlies; things you see under stones, beetles, cockroaches. I have seen cockroaches in Paris as long as my hand. Admittedly I was jagging myself up with Pernod at the time. But I am mortally afraid of all that crawls. I once saw David Attenborough up to his waist in creepie crawlies in a dark cavern and had to throw up in the toilet. I get cardiac arrests, for heaven's sake, if I turn a page of a magazine to find my hand resting on a photograph of an insect.

Dear God, it gets worse than mere insects. I am scared of eels, crabs, snakes, lobsters, (unless à la thermidor and well dead), lizards, crocodiles, alligators, (unless done as watchstraps or trouser belts. I am not even sure of them as handbags). What you have got on your hands here is the Urban Feartie and I don't – Jesus, yes I do – mind admitting it. I am sure that all those amateur psychologists are already identifying me right now as a latent homo with a fear of sex and strong oedipal tendencies but, faced with snakes and silverfish and slaters and all the alien-looking creatures of the deep, I will admit to anything. And as the very repository of machismo I will have to admit to Fear, naked and bold as brass.

Accidental things
December 1985

This column is not a good idea and I am tempting Fate altogether. You know how you suddenly spy your cap/scarf/gloves/umbrella and think: 'I have had THAT a long time'. You view this with smug surprise. 'It's amazing', you think, 'that I have not already lost or mislaid or burnt holes in this possession with lit cigarette ends'. It is when you suddenly become conscious of the longevity of ownership that the partnership between yourself and your possession is going to be dissolved very shortly. I don't know why this is, but it is. Fate is always round the corner when you start thinking about the blighter. Fate is a curmudgeonly old sod, and this column is nothing but a temptation to the chap. It is not a good idea at all. I am calling disaster upon myself. Today's drivel is about accidents.

There is personal danger in even talking about accidents, and all the more if you are going to state that it is a long time since you had one. It is a long time for me all the same, but I used to be in the thick of them all the time. When I was fifteen or so I was so prone to accidents that I asked the careers officer if there were jobs available in the filed file field. It seemed the only thing I was good at. I fell over so many tables that my legs looked as though I had four sets of kneecaps I was that bruised. I fell over and off almost anything at all.

I fell off walls, wash-houses, and air-raid shelters. I had done this for years. In fact I fell off everything until I was old enough to go a bike, when I fell off that instead. I was a positive expert at falling off the daft big lassies bike which Yvonne next door gave me when she married a capstan lathe operator with a

77

hare lip who took her off to Australia to start a new life. I fell off his bike going round corners, but only when there was gravel on the road, and you had to spend three hours picking stones out of your knee with a needle and painting yourself with gentian ointment like some ancient Pict adorning himself with woad. Oh, I was your man for accidents. When I was fifteen I was at a professional level.

I remember at fifteen trapping my thumb in a rail train door. It was a simple thing to do: very little expertise was required. I merely placed my thumb twixt door and jamb. The real professionalism comes with one's response to such an act of idiocy. I opened the slammed door and extricated my mis-shapen digit. It was, I recollect, a little rosier in hue: a faint flush appeared. I took the thumb along to an adjacent seat where five fellow passengers already sat, pretending that absolutely nothing had happened. They sat there and nonchalantly turned over the business pages of their *Glasgow Heralds*. I think one of them might even have started to light his briar. I sat down next to a middle-aged gentleman in a Dunn's thornproof tweed suit. I uttered not one word. Not one cry; not one bleat. A stoic. (Dear God I was the same at Stalingrad, back in the old days). I sat there as the train pulled out of the station and looked on and watched my nail despondently slide off my thumb on to the cigarette-strewn floor. There didn't seem much that I could do about it. Perhaps it was the shock. In fact the only thing I was capable of doing at all is what I did. I threw up over the fellow passenger's thorn-proof tweed suit. Doubtless today you can casually wrap your nail in a paper hanky and get it sewn back on or something. Back then I was a lot more concerned with the cleaning bill for Mr. Thorn-Proof Tweed Suit. Priorities came differently when I was a lad.

I thought of the thumb incident but recently when I found Big Cairnduff's wife strolling about with what looked like an actual splint on her right thumb. She was also limping faintly. The limp turned out to be the result of her just recent tetanus shot. The wounded thumb was the consequence of an encounter with a corned beef tin. It turned out that young Sharon had torn a lump out of her thumb the night before due to her lack of experience with that daft key thing which corned beef tins employ. I put it to the lady that the lack of expertise might actually have been due to an over acquaintance with gin and Indian tonic water on the night in question. Sharon was deeply affronted at this suggestion, partly, I suspect, because it was probably true. I know corned beef tins. And sardine tins. Any tins at all really. It is a simple fact: you will never inflict the slightest cut open yourself when opening tins at night unless there is a slight impairment caused by bevvy. There is no point at all in Sharon's protestations.

But Mrs Cairnduff was not the only one to suffer an accident this week. A colleague of mine was bragging but a fortnight ago that he had never had any accident at all in his car. Not even a tiny one. Not a scrape, not a mark upon his bumper. Not a single rear light cracked. I tried to stop the colleague from pursuing this ruinous line of thought. Fate has a terrible way of taking you literally. It rises to all temptation. In the case of my friend and colleague Fate rose like a star in the sky. It gave him two accidents one after the other. The first was when he backed into a bollard in the school playground. Admittedly these bollards were designed by the crazed architect to jump out and hit the backs of cars for spite. In the other accident an over-keen lady seemed to have tried to get through a space about the size of an eye of a needle, bumping into the colleague's car. No damage seems to have been done but that is not the point.

The point is that my fellow dominie had brought it all upon himself. Fate is waiting out there for you, listening for every rash remark and boast. I know this column is not a good idea. I will be losing my bunnet next and at least one pair of gloves. I am on the look out for the impending accident as well.

Things that break   *October 1985*
Even the Anglepoise lamp which I stole, part by part, from Edinburgh College of Art these many years ago, has decided to

give up. 'Ping' it went, and I knew the lightbulb was dead. I put a new bulb in. It went ping too. I buggered up three screws with the wrong screwdriver and sort of re-wired the plug and put in at least six different amp fuses. Nothing worked. I even tried to test the wires. Not a light was cracked. The thing is dead. Finished. I knew it all along: I should have stolen a later model.

It is not the only bit of domestic machinery to have put in its resignation in the last weeks. Practically every light-bulb in the house has decided to go on strike. The switches don't work. The 'fridge died on me last month and lay in a pool of inexplicable water for three days. The tumble drier didn't dry; in fact it stopped tumbling as well. Don't even talk to me about the almost brand new steam iron. Good God, it is only nine years old. For some reason or another it can only go from stone cold to hot enough to weld stainless steel. Nothing works at all in this house of mine any more: I reckon I've got a football teams' worth of bloody poltergeists in here. The bloody pedal bin won't pedal, the kitchen roll holder fell off, the Hoover sprays dust everywhere like a damned insecticide helicopter across the American prairies. The only electric fire blew up a fortnight ago and the central heating hasn't worked since last November. Dear God, even the toilet seat has a crack across it and, if you are not deeply careful it gives your bum a nasty nip upon rising. This house of mine is falling apart.

The domestic has of course been pointing out these drawbacks to a happy home-life but, until recently, I have not bothered my silly little head about such prosaic matters. It is only a house after all: I use it simply to sleep and keep my shaving stuff in. The final straw was the crack in the toilet seat. A nipped bum is no laughing matter.

I am not happy about the Anglepoise lamp either. When I think of the lengths I went to in thieving it – taking wee daft screws and things home in my little knapsack and eventually, with difficulty, assembling all the bits together – I am upset beyond belief at the notion of having to actually buy a new one.

We are now talking about a new refridgerator, a new Hoover, a new washing machine. I will doubtless have to invest in a new iron, an at least recent ironing table, an electric fire which works. I forgot to tell you about the cooker. That works no bother: that works only too well and all the rings go on at full blast when I only switch one on. The toaster refuses to eject the toast and you can't get the damned bread out of it except by applying a kitchen knife to it. I shall probably be electrocuted in the next month with one hand upon the breadknife and the other poised over the Golden Shred. I am probably the only citizen in the whole of the U.K. who has to wear rubber-soled shoes to have breakfast. Nothing works; the centre cannot hold, everything falls apart. I am beginning to fall apart a bit myself.

Buttons are falling off my cashmere coats. Somebody is going about my entire wardrobe while I am asleep and fraying through every thread which comes anywhere close to a button. Hardly a coat, jacket, blazer, or shirt is unaffected by this blaggards nocturnal exercises. Shoes are getting holes in them and heels fall off at will. Neckties fray for no reason at all, and socks sprout instant holes. Sometimes external agencies are at work. I have but recently jammed by best Burberry in a taxi door, leaving a long, dark, oily stripe across the hem. God knows what those robbers of dry-cleaners will charge to erase the stain – if, that is – they can ERASE it: I will probably have to invest in a new raincoat. I will probably have to go bare-shouldered. I will probably die of bloody pneumonia because of constant drenching. Incidentally, my television set doesn't work and this very typewriter ribbon is so faint it looks as if I am typing a Gestetner stencil. I forgot to mention that the poncie wee gold chain that I used to wear around my poncie wee wrist has a broken catch. Everything around me is less healthy than I am, which is to say that the world is practically at an end. If my watch goes I am going to kill myself.

You realise why this is all happening to me. Why everything is falling apart. I will guarantee that every one of you lot out there are well used to that phenomena of propinquity twixt poverty and demands made upon your income. In short, chaps, your Urban V is broke, stony, strapped for cash. When I put my hands in my pockets all I find is fingers. THAT is why everything is breaking down, why there is this positive intumescence, my dears, of domestic mayhem. When you are in poverty everything assembles for the final coup: you haven't got a chance.

The reason why the Urban Voltaire is without the price of a drink almost, let alone the cash to repair the household goods is that the Inland Revenue has got him in its clutches. Since the beginning of August they have been sending me daily letters demanding money with menaces. I am not kidding you about the menaces. I get weekly injunctions to pay all sorts of sums within the next seven days otherwise they are going to visit me at three in the morning, shoot me in my bed, and take me off to the nearest police station/hospital, handcuffed and still in my underpants. It is clear to me that they have got the wrong man. As far as I can see the way that the tax authorities are abrading a perfectly respectable citizen such as your man here, they must be thinking that I am in the actual Mafia. The last person to be as harrassed by income tax wallahs was Al Capone.

There is absolutely no point in telling these people that I have not got a penny in the world. The chaps are merciless. There is absolutely no value in explaining that I don't have a scooby-doo what all the numbers they keep writing about actually are. According to the Inland Revenue it is a statutory offence to fail to possess a degree in Calculus and a post-grad in Fiscal Accountancy. I am thinking of emigrating on a false passport and getting to hell out of it.

It is not just the daily letter in the buff envelope which is getting to me: there are the buttons falling off, the fraying ties, the emergent holes in the hose, the washing machine, the stove, the electrical wiring. It is all getting on top of me. The final one was the Anglepoise lamp which I stole, part by part, from Edinburgh College of Art. Symbolic it was. The light is inexorably going out of my life, and I am not sure if I can find my way homewards.

Knickers ... or pants

IT was Miss Bringham, the infant mistress, who started me off in my keen and abiding interest in girls' pants. Fixing the small girls at morning assembly with a stern eye (she had two stern eyes but had a tendency to use one at a time), she informed the lassies that they were not under any circumstances to reveal even a whisper of their drawers. Until this point I had regarded lassies linen of no consequence whatsoever. Miss Bringham's injunction immediately changed that. A small girl with hair the colour of a cornfield and eyes like bluebells in spring turned to me wickedly and showed her pants in seconds.

There were a thousand Miss Bringhams and maybe more all over the British Isles in those days and there are still a right good squad of them to this day. I am not sure I disagree with their strictures anyway: if there is one delicious aspect of sexuality, it is strictures.Once it stops being naughty you might as well regard sex as much the same as going to the lavvy. Some folk do.

A wee touch of sin helps us all along. He who is without sin is probably too feart to cast a clout, let alone a stone, and there would be little fun in breathing. Thank goodness I take a drink. Look at they Arabs. The chaps are currently inflamed by Irn Bru: if they took a wee refreshment they would get things in proportion. Sin is your very man, and I am all for it. I digress. Let us go back to girls' pants.

And a grand word pants is too, redolent as it is of the most splendid prohibitions. The Yanks call trousers pants and have ruined it. Mind you, panties is quite nice. Knickers would have you greeting with lust. Bloomers is no good at all.

My old grandma used to adjust her dress outside the

stairheid toilet, and a most uncomfortable sight it was too, her tucking her chemise into a pair of pink flannel bloomers which resembled nothing other than an inner tyre for the wheel off a lorry. No doubt in her Edwardian girlhood she had the grandfather salivating at the sight of a well-turned calf, but bloomers always struck me as somehow unwomanly. A nice pair of panties are a different matter however.

A different matter they are indeed this weather. You are not entirely going to believe this but it is true: the weemenfolk have taken to doing daft things to their underwear. They have taken to designing such items themselves.

"In 1990," says a recent article in a posh blatt, "it is women who are designing underwear for women." And what, well, an arse they seem to be making of it too. Aparrently Godber's range of practical cotton-lycra briefs, bras, and something, dear readers, called bodysuits, is outselling everything else at a shop called Knickerbox.

A bint called – what else – Bianca Maria is responsible for the range of undergarments which are "clean, modern, and functional". I would hope they would be clean myself, but "modern" means, as the word always does, spurious and absurd; and functional, as regards underwear, reminds one a little unnecessarily I should have thought that the function of underwear is to soak up sweat and other, worse, bodily secretions.

I do not want ladies wearing functional panties, I want them sporting pants with an entirely different function from the function of my underwear, and I suspect that most sensible women will be thinking the same as myself at that.

Says this ludicrous article in this ludicrous blatt: "The modern woman no longer wants to be trussed up in flirtatious flounces and itchy lace like a tantalising package."

It gets worse. The harpie who scrawled this mince also says "Women have become more self-confident and want underwear that is no nonsense comfortable." I know exactly what this drivel is leading to, with its confident women and non-flirtatious clean modernity. I have seen the range of cotton and lycra garments and I will tell you that the confident modern bloody bricklayer has probably got more lace on his drawers than this functional rubbish possesses.

I know what this is all about. It is about feminists wanting to be men. They already dress themselves in trousers and cavort around like ageing tomboys, and a most unlovely sight it is at that. Now they want to wear Y-fronts and semmits.

The next thing you know the crazed termagants will be cutting their tits off and trying to grow sticky out bits. If you think that's offensive, think of another offence entirely. Think of the offence to the majority of women. By far the majority of girls and women rather prefer being made the way they are and rather like being feminine, even if it means flirtatious flounces rather than a cotton and lycra bloody bandage round their nether parts.

I have never heard anything so daft. Well I have really. I have heard the same daftness for many a long feminist year now. And it was just as daft when poor old Miss Bringham tellt the lassies in the infant class that the sight of a pair of pants should be denied the boys just out of badness. Nice word that too. Bad.

Black things *1st Feb 1991*

Black may very well be the colour of your true love's hair but that is no reason why it should also be the colour of every damned garment she shoves on her back. Mind you. I have not the slightest objection to the lassies sportings black undies – in a discreet fashion you understand – but I am beginning to tire horribly of every slip of a girl bouncing about in the most negative hue one can think of.

For the truth is, if you have not noticed, is that black is the colour of fashion these days. Black, black, and Bible black, as the poet has it. The weemenfolk this weather have decided, and for some time too, to wear the colour of mourning at all times. It is not a colour for a pretty girl. In fact, it is not a colour at all.

In the theory of light, white is all the colours mixed together.

More Bedside Urban Voltaire

It doesn't work in pigment. I can yet remember trying the theory out in the art class at school immediately following one of Pete Bell's dramatic chemistry lessons (they were dramatic quite simply because Peter taught physics and his chemistry was shaky enough for his little charges to enjoy many a glorious disaster with Leibich Condensers and the like).

It didn't work with the paint and all you got was a sort of mud and the wrath of the art teacher. All the colours are colours, and then there's hues and shades and tints and tones and pastel colours and bright colours and primary colours and, anyway, lots of colours. But, black is not a colour. It is the colour, in fact, of an absence of light.

It is when you are a city boy for the first time in the country and realise that there are no streetlights and it is pitch dark and you are practically soiling your drawers with the sheer eeriness of all this black. It is when your mum put out the bedlamp and left you to the demons of the evening umbra. It is when people die. It is not only not a colour: it is an omen of evil and dark thoughts. But the girls have chosen it.

I have seen this phenomenon before. I recollect that the colour for girls not so long back was mulberry. I can remember turquoise (and an especially grisly fashion was for purple and lilac; on a pale girl with flaxen hair the effect was straight out of an Edgar Allan Poe story). But black goes one further. The only woman it would suit would be a rich widow: Listen: a paper bag would suit a rich widow.

You cannot move in this land without seeing some splendid wee bird dressed up like a 45-year-old Italian matron. I have been threatening the girls in Babbity Bowster's boozer for some time with buying them all pink frocks. I look at all these splendid girls and think to myself how pretty they must have looked when their parents dressed them. If I was their dads I'd be keeping them in for going about dressed up as Islamic fundamentalists. "And put a decent bloody dress on you before you go out of my house!" I'd be shouting. The girls are jouking about clad in the sort of gear which Max Wall used for an intended comic effect. And for why? For why, I'd like to know.

Badness, that's what it is. Just out of sheer badness is the reason. There was a time when the women dressed themselves up to look attractive to the menfolk. Now that they can jaunt around earning a living for themselves they don't have to pull in the guys. Well, they do really, but they can pretend they don't. At first it was simple. They made themselves intentionally ugly with shorn locks and dungarees. Then they took to dressing to please themselves and other women. And eventually it came to the black, the very nullification of colour, of daylight, of life itself. Like the Cimmerians, the lassies now want to spend their lives in the dark.

I'm in the dark about it myself in a way. Men are somehow not permitted to clad themselves in anything other than greys and navys and murky browns.

Wee Brendan McLaughlin of the Scotia Bar shows off from time to time in scarlet or pink or viridian, suits and why not? You should hear the catcalls he attracts from the lieges in the street. But dammit he's right at that. Al Capone was wont to attire himself in peppermint suits. I'm all for it. I want the women to take a leaf out of both wee gangsters' – I beg your pardon, Brendan, it just came out that way – books.

A splash of pastel and a sticky-out frock would not come amiss at all. But the girls are determined on the black. Wandering into the sort of smart wine bar where the modish females go to be cynical about men is like entering bloody Erebus.

Black is also the colour that the Arab women wear when they are out of the house. Inside it they dress themselves in a manner which would make Joan Collins look dowdy, and Western gear it is. The Iranian revolution might have the ladies looking like Rank Bajin in the street but it has not stopped them getting assembled with the best of the Paris chiffon gowns when they are inside in their own domiciles.

Our lassies are under no such constraint but insist on parading themselves in positively tenebrific garments which would do credit to a mujahidin wifie married to a Wee Free minister in sabbath mood. I'm fed up with all this black. I'm raging against it. Rage, rage, against the dying of the light.

Words

Quotes
29th Nov 1985

'Classical quotation is the parole,' said Dr. Johnson, 'of literary men all over the world.' It is a damned good quote at that except that my own grasp of classical quotation would seem to put an end to its sense, but to hell with that.

The word 'parole' incidentally – and I patronise here the younger reader – is used as meaning the notion of passwords. Thomas Love Peacock never wrote a more Augustan dod of prose for an introduction than that, I aver. Your man Thomas Love was fond of a quote himself and here is one of his own: 'A book that (sic) furnishes no quotations is, me judice, a plaything.'

I know what this one-time chief examiner of the East India Company (see the things I know) was getting at. It is this: you can't make up everything out of your own head. Sometimes it is sadly necessary to give credit where credit is due. It is then that you let your chums know that it wisnae you who said it first: it is another mortal's glory in which you bask when it comes to good phrase.

I have another quotation for you and there is not a reason in the world why it should not stand for your Urban Voltaire. 'Next to the originator of a good sentence,' wrote none other than Ralph Waldo Emerson, 'is the first quoter of it.' In the absence of a decent quotation being accredited to myself that will have to do I suppose.

There is indeed a definite absence in this area in Mr Alan Bold's most recent offering. Let me explain. Mr Bold in an inveterate compiler and an anthologiser of repute and the chap resides in Fife, which as you know, is a long, long way from this city of mine. In fact, Mr Bold has anthologised so much of everything *(The Penguin Book of Socialist Verse, The Marital Muse, The Bawdy Beautiful...* sure, it goes on forever), that I shall not be surprised if Boldy does anthologies of such sensitive belles lettres as, for instance suicide notes, correspondence from bank managers, and working-class message lines. Especially the last.

Anyway, Alan has come up with another means of making a right few bob... yet another essential addition to the colourful world of book readin' and the like: A brand new volume entitled *Scottish Quotations*. It is a splendid idea altogether.

The blurb says that this new book 'gathers together some of the most memorable things that have been said by Scots and about Scotland,' and it also says that 'Though ostensibly a small nation of 5,000,000 souls, Scotland is a large subject.' Boldy is, if he doesn't mind me mentioning it, actually a larger subject himself than this shilpit wee bit of obsequious bog and some of the very best quotes – invariably from the cultured pens of Englishmen – seem much in keeping with that sentiment. What I am pointing to about this volume is the absence, on the whole, of decent quotes.

The old Everymans quotations dictionary has more than 10,000 quotations and proverbs, while the new edition of the Oxford has nearly twice that. The *Scottish Quotations* anthology has a mere 500 of the blighters. Few of them are memorable and most of them are daft though I am bound to say that the most surprising chaps have been well-quotable. The original of the publishing house which owns this very blatt you would take for a crusted Tory and a fine, upstanding, Presbyterian greetin' faced old teetotallar but stay your prejudice a while. Was it none other than old George Outram, born in 1805 who sang:

He found that learnin' fame,
Gas, philanthropy, an' steam,
Logic, loyalty, gude name,
Were a' mere shams;
That the source of joy below,
And the antidote to woe,
An' the only proper go,
Was drinkin' drams.

Mind you, Geordie croaked at the age of 51, doubtless through such a hedonistic notion, but I am glad to see that his philosophy has been religiously observed, by his employees at any rate ever since.

I was after telling you about the absence of decent quotes: it is true. I am not in it myself. Not a single word from my frequent fulminations upon Highlanders, heedies, the General Assembly of the Church of Scotland, or the ruinous price of drink in this tome. I am in good enough company here however. I can find only three out-and-out politicians being quoted in the entire book. (I do not count Cunninghame-Graham, who was an Argentine cowboy; indeed John McLean himself is probably here more as a part of Scottish literary myth.)

From a land which has produced damn-near every radical of note since the birth of the beginning of the nineteenth century and five Prime Ministers this century it seems a trifle odd to include quotes from W Hamilton and another from the absurd Nicholas Fairbairn.

It is, yet, a decent wee book, and pleasant enough to sift through looking for something suitable to write a column around. There are just too many Edinburgh New Townees with literary pretensions around the pages and such literateurs are not of the most popular stamp at that.

No book of Scottish quotations should, for instance, be without the immortal phrase of Para Handy's. 'If Dougie wass here, he would tell you,' not to mention his positively existential: 'I am 49 years of age; not counting the year I spent in the sawmill.'

True, a couple of the Glaswegerati are in it and Alasdair Gray and Archie Hind are represented well and rightly. But never mind, 'it is a good thing for an uneducated man to read books of quotation,' as Churchill had it.

It is a pity that this Scottish book could have done with better ones, and quotes that said more about Scotland at that. That has ever been the problem with the Scots though. 'Parole, parole, nothing but words,' said the Riccio of Mary Queen of Scots, 'the Scots will boast but rarely perform their brags.'

Real words *12th Oct. 1984*

'Correct me if I am wrong,' said Mr. MacPhail, head teacher of English, with the air of one who has been neither corrected, nor wrong, in 30 years, 'but it would seem to me that the general decline in standards of syntax is but an ineluctable reflection of the moral and...' The English teacher began to warm to his subject. 'Furthermore,' Mr. MacPhail droned on, 'I charge these authorities, videlicet – the Regional...' He continued grandiloquently, his fat fingers resting not inelegantly on the broad sweep of the lapels of his Dunn's thornproof tweed jacket, the breast pocket of which sprouted copious numbers of red Biros.

'Yeah,' said Cameron absently as he peered at Miss Robertson's rather tasty knees through a rolled-up copy of 'The Extended Curriculum: A Strategy.'

The English principal began to expand inexorably on his thesis in front of an assistant head who was trying to work out a computer programme by which every member of staff could be timetabled for compulsory physical jerks. A small officious-looking fellow with thin strands of hair slicked across his pompous skull sat nearby writing a draft of a letter which started: 'From the EIS representative to all members: A people's court has been set up for those who scabbed last Thursday week...'

The English principal was in full flight. 'I fail to see therefore how even an imbecile...', he was explaining as he sprayed the remains of his last sandwich over Miss Watt who had been steadfastly maintaining that education should spring out of the cultural mores enjoyed by the third year catering boys class, and that structuralist conceptualisation showed clearly the efficacy of such an approach.

The teacher supposed to teach modern studies was closely examining the question of the media as a teaching aid, that is to say, he had found two definites for Newmarket that afternoon. He was also musing how Miss Watt could talk such dangerous nonsense when she had such beautiful tits.

The Urban Voltaire allowed all of what passed for staff room debate to wash softly over his Queen Elizabeth Silver Jubilee mug of Blend 37, and over the wafting smoke from his cigarette, and over his softened brain. His brain felt tender and squashy through prolonged contact with the sort of working-class vitality enjoyed by numbers of small boys and girls in the one room at the one time. 'The death of a thousand cuts,' thought the unhappy schoolmaster, 'must be like this.'

The pointless discussion rolled over the Urban V like a cerebral herbal shampoo. He could hear the orotund catchwords of the English teacher sliding past his consciousness. Words like 'syntax' and 'questions of register' were disappearing into the ether.

As the words took shape, like smoke rings above my head, I began gradually, to remember days past when such matters concerned me. Slow, sleepy, afternoons when the arcane mysteries of English grammar were revealed. I remembered Murphy, who sat beside me and who could do bloody calculus when he was three for heaven's sake but for whom parsing a sentence contained the sort of helplessness I would have when confronted with putting the parts of a Bren gun together.

For me though, grammar was one of the few things in school which made any sense at all. Oh, I was the very man for adverbial clauses of consequence, for the old pronouns and gerunds. No bother for your man here either in the figure of speech game. For a start, figures of speech had such splendid titles. Syne doche ('the pen is mightier than the sword'), or litotes ('No mean city') or – the best of all – zeugma (which, if I recollect rightly, is the use of the possessive before a gerund.) If creatures like the valence table in chemistry, or propositions in geometry, were ferocious wild animals in the torrid jungles of these subjects, then such things as gerunds and metaphors were furry little pets you could caress and call to your side.

Ah, but those are long days past all right. Were I to have my bum at a school desk now there would be no more wee gerunds scampering about. Oh, the grammar is out. Said a spokesman from the Department of Education and Science recently: 'It does not matter if a student can't spell or punctuate: what matters is whether or not he can communicate.'

Punctuate? Today's modern lad or lass couldn't even spell it.

More Bedside Urban Voltaire

The modern student of English now enjoys a fun-packed session of colouring things in, or giving one word answers to interpretations taken from washing machine manuals and other such bilge considered 'relevant' to their boring little lives. I swear the above is true. There exists a book called Real Life Reading Skills. It contains riveting information about how to mend a fuse, or peel a potato. Now you know where the modern novelist gets his ideas from. Devil the bit of literature you'll be getting in the schools today. I caught a Head of English once, putting sets of David Copperfield and Middlemarch in the bin destined for the cleansing department. A bookburner, I call him.

And it is not just your atavistic Urban Voltaire who is reviled by notions of what calls itself literacy this weather. Was it not but the other day that the Head of English at Hutchie Grammar, no less, was saying the same thing and garnering in his support the report by Her Majesty's Inspectorate? But Hutchie Grammar is right wing and elitist and where the bosses send their own weans, isn't it? Well it is, and no wonder come to that. The pity is that the weans of the proletariat are fobbed off instead with illiteracy and ignorance in the guise of fashions and fads.

The literati   *May 1985*

So the Prof has shot the craw. No doubt the prof, to whom I refer, a Mr Colin McCabe, will have difficulty with that last sentence and all the post-structuralist semeiological literary linguistics with which Mr McCabe has packed his curriculum vitae and his heid will not make the phrase any the clearer but shot the craw is what our academic has done. Mr McCabe got the bullet from his former employers, none other than Cambridge Yooni, a set of shocking reactionaries who preferred not to have his brand of pseudo-Marxist gobbledegook littering the quads. At once the old Tech came to the rescue and employed him as a professor, which is a bit like Real Madrid taking on a free transfer from Alloa Athletic and then making

94

him captain. Less than four years after, did not your noble scholar, having brought the team down to the second division, bugger off to a new and more prestigious position with the British Film Institute. What, you may well ask, did Strathclyde University get out of this structuralist boffin? Not a lot, I should think.

Mr McCabe, unless I have got it wrong, seems to be one of a long line of academics who regard their inflated salaries as emoluments for warming their bums at the fire of literary complacency. Where was McCabe, for instance, all these four years? Why did I fail to find him at book launches, book fairs, literary functions, each intended to proselytize books, writers, reading and stuff like that? Mr McCabe, in fact, was in China and Australia for a large part of his employment in Strathclyde University. For the last nine bloody months he wasn't even warming his bum at a Scottish venue: he spent all that time turning a dollar in the U.S. of A., lecturing there, instead of here. Prof. McCabe, it is said, is unhappy about the future of higher education in this country. Neither am I, if it comes to that, if the tarts of academe like McCabe are anything to go by; the good-time girls and guys ready to hop into any academic bed for any sugar-daddy.

Professor McCabe revealed what he had got out of his sojourn with the natives up in Caledonia. Says the man: 'I came up with a certain amount of interest in the Scottish Renaissance but very little other knowledge. I've become increasingly interested in contemporary Scottish writing, writing of which I was completely unaware.' It is hard to imagine what kind of interview the fellow gave when he was appointed literary supremo at Strathclyde Yooni, but, myself, I wouldn't appoint a bloke who told me in advance that he knew damn all about the product he was selling or the clients either. Mr McCabe was then quoted thus: 'novelists', he said, 'such as Alasdair Gray and Jim Kelman just do not have the recognition they should have outside Scotland'.

Alasdair Gray's books sell inexplicably well. The foremost

critic perhaps in the English-speaking world rather ludicrously described Gray as: 'the finest Scottish writer since Sir Walter Scott'. The question whether Gray or Kelman are insufficiently recognised outside of their native land is absurd. The real question is whether they deserve the recognition they have here. For they are a sorry lot, the Scottish Literati.

Oh, there is lots of innocent, knockabout, fun to have with the Scottish literati. Most of them look extremely odd for instance. It is a photographer's nightmare trying to get Alasdair to look sane, let alone literary. Gray has owlish glasses held together with Sellotape, 1950's Burton suits smeared with beer-stains and breakfast egg, a straggly moustache, demented hair, erratic gestures, and a manic laugh. Archie Hind is as thin as Ghandi and sports the sort of grey beard which makes one muse upon the sort of chin beneath it. Liz Lochead is plump with doleful spaniel eyes, Tom Leonard limps, Alan Bold looks like an especially complicated Rubik's Cube and shaves his facial hair in such a manner as to imply insanity. Alex Hamilton is two doubtful eyes set in a ball of hair, and Willie McIlvanney is so film-starringly gorgeous that you want to know exactly what he is sublimating by his writing. The bloody lot of them make my cover-up hairstyle look positively normal.

But this is all superficial, knockabout, fun. There are charges to be put to the Scottish writers whom Professor McCabe has but recently discovered. The first charge is that the scribes are not as good as they are thought to be. Alasdair Gray, for instance, lionised as he is, has his critics. Many there are to vaunt his genius: few there are who have actually finished his books. The only way to read his stuff is the way he wrote it all: in bits. The suspicion remains that the strangeness of Gray's prose, ideas, persona, and appearance, is his skeleton key to literary approval. Afraid they are, the critics, to voice their bewilderment in case they appear stupid. There is a terrible cachet in pretending to know what Alasdair is talking about, like laughing at jokes in French films before the subtitles come up.

If you think Alasdair is a touchstone for the subtle mind, wait till Glasgow writer Farquhar McLay's latest book comes out. He writes in bloody Runic. The intelligentsia will enjoy that.

But Gray and the rest of them belong, against their wishes I agree, to coterie artiness, a sort of cultural sewing bee, knitting myths to send, like khaki socks, to the lads in the front line of Scottish consciousness. Thus do we have the interminable anthologies of Glasgow short stories, poems, musings, ready for the 'O' Grade class, relevant and couthy and just the stuff for lefties in Social Work and the Hyndland Road to agree with.

Out of all this outpouring of the West of Scotland literati is the sort of Scottishness which would make you greet. They deny the Highlander on the shortbread tin and the heather on a dancer's dress on an STV show and replace it all with Benny Lynch and Red Clydeside and tattie scones, Johnnie Stark and razor slashers, high rise flats and the Old Firm, the colours they were fine, excoriate the Pope and Pass the Ammunition.

The critic Douglas Gifford recently maintained in a publication: 'There is a Scottish fictional tradition,' he wrote, 'but that tradition is precisely about the writers' repeated sense of their being no tradition'.

I am tired of all this search for a tradition, this search for the Dear Green Place that Archie Hind set up as a chimera long years ago. Writers are people and not locations and you will not find art or life upon an Ordnance Survey map. While our writers are looking for their own voice and their own traditions they should cast an eye, and envious a one at that, upon a tradition on our doorsteps. The tradition of the Englishman on the make, just like the one who came up here four years ago, and who is shooting the craw right now and smartish.

Sunday supps *April 1989*

There is nothing like a glossy magazine – even a non-glossy one if it comes to that – for bringing you back to reality. Magazines bring such a process about by simply inverting reality. Stand whatever a magazine has to say on it's head and it is astonishing how much better it balances in this new posture. Magazines exist quite simply to be bought and for no other reason. Why people buy them – and women do so in their droves, my dears – is another matter. Why people actually glimpse through the pages of the mags is through sheer boredom I should think. It must be ennui which causes myself to turn over the leaves of the drivel they insert into the posh Sunday blatts.

One of the Sunday blatts is currently shoving in a magazine within a magazine. This is some sort of photography supplement. It exists as a super wheeze to get chaps to go out and throw a grand away on cameras and lenses which they will then use to take snaps of lacteous mums and salivating infants and other such sickening displays of consanguineous sentimentality. This week's snap supp was devoted to landscape. What splendidly artistic photos there were too. Made the very most of the strangeness of the world around us they did. The problem was really that not one single arty snap displayed a spot of the old scenic vistas which you would ever in a million years want to visit. They were each thrilling pictures of mudflats, boulders, moorland: one got the curious impression that the photographers had searched the world for interesting views and ended up poking their lenses at Stevenson beach, (ha), in December. It is hard for philistines like myself to grasp the beauty of Stevenson beach in any month, but there you are.

Now I only squinted through this snappers guide to affectation but I took a little longer over the main mag of this blatt. There was a riveting piece about a father and daughter. I read this every week in mounting disbelief. The sons and daughters always love their mums and dads and are proud of them being ever so famous. (It is only famous mums and dads who are featured, as one might expect).

The sons always remember a fearful row from dad when they went off on their own to Tunisia at the age of seventeen and smoked dope till their heads fell off but it is all right now because they are doing this super job which daddy got them running a theatre in Chichester. In the daughter's cases neither the mum or dad ever seems to have been worried when she got expelled from school at fourteen and went to live with a West Indian actor. I don't know what the upper-class is coming to. Instead of the old Victorian values and cold showers every morning it seem that the weel-aff are determined to make their weans insufferable to their own kind as well as to us. The lefty-liberal weel-aff are, as you might expect, the worst. You should have seen the stoatirs the Sunday supp came up with last week.

Alan Coren is a former editor of Punch and a media chap in all ways and was once a very left wing fellow indeed, which did not stop him from sending his brats, (Giles and Victoria he named them) to the best of the private schools and entertain their infant lives with a succession of nannies. His daughter Victoria is sixteen years of age and her daddy says that 'although she has the carapace of cynicism which shows in her writing, she is very soft-hearted and cries easily'. I will tell you this: if she was my sixteen year old daughter she would be greetin' very easily indeed and often, with a well-skelped ear to go to bed with every night especially if she possessed the sort of arrogant self-assurance which Mr Coren has clearly thrust upon his young Victoria.

But it would be as nothing to the skelped ears of Mr Coren himself, who deserves them bitten off by a football hooligan for this wee gob of mince: 'I identify with Victoria because she pursues the same trade as I do' or 'The sheer fecundity of her literary imagination is overwhelming'. Miss Coren is sixteen and attends St. Paul's School. She also writes a column for the Weekend Section of the Daily Telegraph. This month her collected articles are to be published. It is possible that Miss Coren, aged sixteen, is practically Percy Byshe Shelley in a dress made out of literary fecundity and it is possible her da had sod all to do with her getting a weekly column in a national newspaper. It is probably my carapace of cynicism which brings about a wee doubt or two in my mind. Maybe she has went to a better school that what I did.

I will not reveal any more of what dad and daughter Coren had to say about each other – and what they had to say about themselves was even worse – there is no reason to spoil your day entirely. Anyway, I cast the mag aside and picked up the Radio Times instead. I imagined a dose of glorious information about what Ken Bruce eats for lunch and the like to cheer me up. There was an article about Robin Day instead in which I gleaned that he had led a strike over Spam rations at his Isle of Wight boarding school and was now the greatest mind the world has ever known and not really a failed politician. I went back to the photo journal supplement. All of a sudden the beaches of Stevenson looked welcoming and far, far, away.

Kids' words? *January 1986*

I owe a debt deeply to the following names which I found enscribed in a wizard prang supersonic hefty-decent little volume the other day. The first name, written in a neat schoolboy hand, was 'Graeme Hood'. The other, legible but less experienced in the calligraphic art, was 'Alasdair Hood'. I owe, for once, debts to several other small visigoths as well as I will soon reveal. But it was the two young chaps just mentioned who told their dad that they agreed with every single word, or at least the ones they could understand no doubt, of my drivel on William books the other week. Bright young fellows I should say. The debt I owe them is this: they asked their father if he thought I would like to be re-introduced to the wizard prang, hefty supersonic book I was telling you about. It was thus that I found once more the company of J.C.T. Jennings.

Jennings and Darbishire. And Venables and Temple, alias Bod. And Mr Carter and Mr Wilkie and Martin Winthrop Barlow Pemberton-Oakes, M.A. (Oxon), Headmaster of Linbury Court Preparatory School. Temple is alias Bod because his initials are C.A.T. so naturally he is called Dog. Dog, it seems, does not have quite the correct ring to it, so he is then called Dogsbody for short. But Dogsbody needs shortening. By this simple process does Temple become Bod and I quite agree. Wizard Prang I call it.

I hadn't really forgotten Jennings: he had just sort of taken a holiday from my mind for a few years. I remember though that they were splendid books though, as a wee boy I had really been more in favour of William. Master Brown had a bit more dash to him, I'd thought then. But Jennings was good too and probably a bit more real in a way because his adventures were set in a school, albeit a very different one from the old Townhead Primary where I was Dux. (Swank – hefty super swank), and William after all lived in a village with a maid and a cook nipping about the house.

But re-reading the adventures of both the young varlets has been a revelation to me. I had forgotten the sheer quality of the writing for a start. I'd forgotten it of course because I never knew it really: I just took it for granted. It is only now that what is left of my raven locks is frosting over and my bonny brow is by no means brent that I can see it. These were books which introduced us to language, ideas, literature, and the kind of general breadth of knowledge now so rare that there are whole television programmes designed to display such an eccentricity. Here are some things which I remember gleaning out of *Jennings Goes to School:* Bubonic Plague, The Spanish Inquisition, Taxidermy, Tarantula spiders, Yashmak veils. That's just for starters. What about the words?

I asked a group of fourth-formers, all on the verge of sitting their 'O' Grades in English, the meaning of words like 'Gargantuan, ensconced, imminent, doughty, sublime, authoritative, ablution, ascertain, sedate, voluminous, characterisation', and 'logically'. All in all there were twenty words. Not one single pupil managed to explain one single word. Mind you, be reasonable, be reasonable. They didn't have a word-processor, whatever that is, with them. No bleeping little screen about to stick chewing gum in their little eyes. The words were too hard, they said. All of them came from *Jennings Goes to School.* Jennings is – was – for children of nine upwards.

I received a positive avalanche, my dears, of letters about that column on the William books, from all sorts of literates including, I can proudly reveal, a Regius Professor, and a prominent Scottish Jurist. And loads of weans put pen to paper. I especially prize the missive from young Laura and Jennifer who finished by wishing me love and threw a row of crosses in for good measure. It proves to me that there are still children alive who can read books with words in them and everything. I'll bet they are the ones whose mums and dads give them books to read.

But as for the weans who don't read books at all – it isn't really their fault at all, is it? It is not, after all, the kids who actually make all those television sets, let alone the bloody television programmes, or the video games, or the ghetto-blasters or any of the meretricious technological baubles which are ever dangled, like a hypnotist's watch, in front of a now largely quiescent population, sated as it is with *Dynasty* and Noel Edmond's shows and fizzy drinks and quick-serve savoury rice.

Naturally all the above are palatable to the undiscriminating mind and palette, requiring neither thought nor sensibility, (nor sense, if it comes to that). Naturally there are apologists for the notion that this is all right anyway. Dear God, I am an elitist swine, I am. I am anyway in response to a recent letter to this very blatt in which a correspondent averred that Latin, Greek, Philosophy, and Sociology are luxuries this country cannot afford. I hope he was being ironic, but I know there are lots of chaps out there who agree with his argument. Nobody who ever read *Jennings* in childhood would though. We know what we would call such a thesis. Ozard, we'd call it. Hefty, hairy, supersonic ozard at that.

French letters
April 1988

I have here in front of me the ultimate in cheek: a newsletter from an organisation purporting to be the University of Stirling. I have been to Stirling and have seen this 'University'.

This blatt's Literary Editor (Ha!) went to this pretension. The place is nothing but a chip shop and a so-called degree from there has about as much substance as Ian Paisley's doctorate which is to say not much or even none at all of any kind. A News Release indeed. Let alone a Yooni.

But this News release suggests that some kind of intellectual activity is going on within the establishment. You should read it for yourself. It is about a new French course. I know, I know: I thought of it myself. A course in French Literature at Stirling Poly MUST be entitled FRENCH LETTERS. (According to this news release Stirling does indeed see its French course in this way. It is a prophylactic rather than a seeding culture.)

Says this ridiculous pronunciamento: 'Students taking the new French course will be asked to read just one book – over and over again'. This is – I can assure you – a direct quote. It goes on too. It turns out that the 'course' is for Master of Philosophy in Modern French Literature. I told you this was the Bob Jones University of Milwaukee or whatever it is – you could get a qualification in picking your nose here. The course at this Stirling farrago is how to be a Master of Modern French Literature starts this September and takes two and half years to complete. Two and a half years.

'I'll never forget the day I read a book' sang Jimmy Durante. It only took Schnozzle a day to read his: it will take two and half days years to read this one. It is, incidentally, 'Madame Bovary'. Gustave Flaubert wrote it and I have read it. Dashed good it is too. Splendid read. Important, influential, seminal as well, (good Yooni word that), chap can't call himself civilised if he hasn't turned the pages of the novel over.

A bloke called Alastair Duncan, also called the 'course director', explains himself in the news release. He says the students are going to read this Madame Bovary – important book by the way – for two and a half years from, he says: 'A variety of points of view, Humanist, Marxist structuralist, etc. It will be the same book,' he states, 'but different every time it is read'. The chap's insane.

More Bedside Urban Voltaire

Mind you the news release tells us that the luckless scholars will 'eventually' get the chance to read other books. 'In fact,' says this raving lunatic of a course director, 'we shall be spending six months on feminist literature'. I do not know if you have ever read 'Madame Bovary'. It is about a neurotic bird who cheats on her fine upstanding husband and who gets her rocks off imagining that the Holy spirit can enter her physically as well as spiritually. When it came out the author was banned from France practically because there is a masturbation scene involving a fantasy with a priest. It is about as feminist as

Now as it turns out I am not too hot on the old Modern French literature. I have read a couple of other novels by the same Monsier Flaubert, and a bit of Zola, and even a touch of my own namesake, your man Voltaire. I have glanced at Dumas (pere and fils), and enlighted at the romance of the Count of Monté Cristo and the hunchback of Nôtre Dame. There is Balzac and Gide and Stendhal. Modern French literature suggests Sartre and Camus and Malraux. Collette wrote some marvellous things. You cannot call yourself educated if you have never encountered the tragedy of Abbe Prevost's *Manon Lescaut*. There is Alain Fournier's *Le grand Mealnes*. Celine, Proust. Poets like Rimbaud, Velaine, Willon, Baudelaire... what am I doing here? I know almost sod all about French literature but I appear to know more than Dr Duncan, course director. I know this: if your boy or girl was about to enrol at a Yooni which told them they were going to read the one book for two and a half years looking at it from, of course, a variety points of view, Humanist, Marxist, structuralist etc., you wouldn't care if they were ending up by colouring the bloody thing in, you would tell your offspring to chuck the studying and go off and get a sensible job.

Where will this all end? 'The students,' medical schools will proclaim 'will study feet for two and a half years, looking at them from,' they will continue, 'a variety of points of view, Humanist, Marxist, structuralist...'. Nuclear physicists will be blowing up half the world because they looked at their book from a Humanist, Marxist... artists will draw the left eye of the model over and over again from a variety of points of view. You fellows out there daft enough to watch the idiot box will be regaled with the same episode of *Neighbours* nightly for the next two and a half decades. One night you'll all be humanists and the next Marxists and a wee dose of structuralists the day after and then on to greater things, supplemented of course by a thorough grounding in Feminism and the menstrual cycle. I give up.

Dispiriting, it is. And the most depressing thing about this fresh burst of academic surrealism is that this came in a News Release. A news release, I ask you. It is one thing for Stirling Yooni to think up something as absolutely bloody silly as this course in French Literature: it is quite another to boast about it.

Irish English   *December 1986*

They made Spencer sit beside me. The notion was that he would improve in his English. This was a crazy idea. Spencer could do Maths, Physics, Calculus, and invent Radium. What he couldn't do was penetrate the mysteries of English grammar. Spencer thought that syntax was a disease that cows got. He imagined a gerund as a small furry animal which was bred in Ross-shire to make stoles for middle-class ladies who went to Works' dinners. He assumed that gerundives were baby gerunds. Spencer was hopeless – inventively hopeless – at English. I was a wizard.

The teacher was Irish accented enough to get called Paddy and Irish-accentuated enough to deserve it. He wrote marvellously literary erratum throughout your ink exercises. I especially admired one of his parting lines at the end of a Spencerian essay. It read: 'You speakum English heap good'. In one of my own more self-important efforts he wrote: 'Enjoyed your novel. Count Tolstoy never had an English teacher. I gave up the marking after the eleventh page. You win.' I didn't understand this at the time: it has taken years. The essay was meant to be of not less than two pages in length. Another time he wrote at the bottom of an especially purplish piece of prose: 'I question your sanity. After reading this I am beginning to question mine'. He was a lovely bloke.

He was also a good teacher if I remember, though he never had what dominies invariably describe as good discipline. Does it matter anyway? Most of the kids who went through his hands over the years didn't bother with English at all: it had the queer smell. Grammar. Syntax. Adverbial clause of How and What and... most of the kids thought clauses were what you ate chips up.

For an Irishman he had a terrible regard for terminological exactitude: he thought words were Truth and created hell if he thought you were abusing the language. 'If the English hoard words like misers,' wrote the late Kenneth Tynan, speaking of the earlier but also late Brendan Behan, 'the Irish spend them like sailors'. Not all of the Irish do, even if they all have love affairs with language, forever caressing the breasts of it, snapping the English language's bra straps, shoving their hands up its skirt. Some of the Irish are dreadfully presbyterian in their approach to language, their own and ours. They like it dressed up and respectable for the morning shopping, as much as they look forward to it wanton for a scarlet night out on the town. Paddy was all for the language in a morning-dress, decent, and fit to see sunlight.

He was, I suspect, an old-fashioned man and none the worse for it and loved Hazlitt and Charles Lamb and Addison and Steele. He introduced me to Thomas Love Peacock, but also to James Joyce. I used to be ashamed of liking all that stuff and many the apostasy I uttered. It wasn't a mere thrice I denied Him, believe me. Paddy's big thing was clear language. I told you he was almost a Presbyterian. He couldn't abide waffle and told you so. Dead these long years back now, he'd have loved this week: getting his own back on the onanists of language. Bureaucrats are the most notorious in this league. That's what The Plain English Campaign say anyway.

The Plain English Society are terribly dull. Like Paddy, my

old mentor, they do not enjoy English at its most surreal. They object to the British Gas shares application document for using the word 'notwithstanding' throughout and suggest that the boring wee mot 'but' would have done just as well instead. But? But? Bureaucrats don't say but, not even at the end of a sentence notwithstanding. Like. The winner of this year's Plain English Society prize demands it even if only for his monicker.

The winner had this to say: 'I would also advise you that if an account has debit interest, this will not accrue to credit interest where the balance is insufficient, i.e., where the balance is less than the debit interest accrueing. The debit interest will in fact increase'. Twas brillig, and the slithy toves did gyre and gimble in the wabe. The bit in quotation marks was written by the assistant district manager of the Halifax Building society: why not? He strikes me as a fine example of a mimsy borogove. You are not going to believe this but the assistant director of the whatever it is called is called Mr Bumstead. Nature is always imitating Art. Charles Dodgson couldn't have done better.

Mr Bumstead got first prize, and so he should. I'll bet they never looked, all the same, at any document penned by Strathclyde Regional Council Education Department. The Council like big words and longer sentences, the dafter the better. The sentence first, and the verdict afterwards is their notion at most times. What's the last line of that Lewis Carroll couple of couplets? 'And the mome raths outgrabe' it is, I seem to remember. There was ever something sinister about Lewis Carroll, which is doubtless his appeal. I was always frightened of all those mome raths outgrabing, in fact, out there at all. Paddy, my old teacher would have known what I was talking about, clearly, when I say that it is the Mr Bumsteads of this world who outgrabe you if they can only get away with it.

Books *12th Oct. 1990*

My life has been ruined by books. Ruined it was when my toddler chums, gaily playing in the street outside, discovered me reading *Coral Island* and could not understand why I refused to enter into their adventures because I was more involved with those of Ralph, Jack, and Peterkin. Today's psychologists could tell you all about my desire to re-enter the womb.

Reading as a very young child is an aberration no doubt, but it is not a kick in the arse off a perversion. My Grandma used to give me old Chatterbox Annuals to read when she had her afternoon nap and they were splendid Edwardian affairs full of pictures of sultry Edwardian misses in lacy petticoats and lovely black stockings and long ringlets and rose-leaf lips and such sadness in their Edwardian eyes as would keep a decent little lad of the late 1940's in masturbation fantasies for a week at least.

When I went to school, my life was ruined by ridiculous women with their hair in tight buns who complained because you went faster in reading a line in the laughably infantile "book" they gave you, than the rest of the class who were clearly made up of the sort of moronic children whom educationists have insisted in calling the less-abled. Less-abled? Some of them were so less-abled they could strip the lead off a roof in less time than it took to recite a Shakespeare sonnet. You could rattle out *Ben Battle was a soldier bold* and they would have the top of a cathedral off you.

My eyesight was ruined by books. I was one of the archetypal legions of bookworms who in childhood read under the bedclothes with a torch. Once my father took the torch away and I used a candle to light up my literacy instead. My brother, who shared the bed, survived, and is ever in the debt of the Burns Unit at Yorkhill Hospital for Sick Children. I had a sore bum for a fortnight. Nobody ever thought of sending me to a hospital.

My academic career was ruined by books. I took to truanting and going to Glasgow's Mitchell Library to read books rather than listen to Chemistry teachers giving me celebrations concerning Leibich Condensers and other arcana of the Sciences. I was wont to spend my dinner money on such occasions on a game of snooker, a swatch round the Kelvingrove Art Galleries, four hours in the library and five Batchelor fags.

My health was ruined by books. It wasn't just squinting at the letters by candlelight under the counterpane and giving me the sort of eyesight enjoyed by mute inglorious Miltons who are resting, it was the ineffable manner by which bookworms such as myself took to incessant cigarette smoking as I began to get actually anxious over what was going to happen to Julien Sorel. And worse. I began to be incapable of reading anywhere else but a public house in the daytime.

My subsequent alcoholism can be seen in a direct line to my student days when I eschewed friends and family in favour of books and beer. Later I came to whisky and whimsy and the sort of wilfulness you develop when you don't meet the sort of people you read about in books. My mental health came to be called into question too.

Mental health. I started putting everybody I met into characters of the real people I met in books. I could tell a Causubon at three paces, at least three aunties were juggled about in Jane Austen novels. I considered my colleagues in terms of whether or not they could be Charley Bates, The Artful Dodger, or Oliver Twist. Every girl I met had to be Estella. It was a lot worse with myself, I varied between Stephen Dedalus and Queequeg, for Christ's sake, it just depended on how much I had to drink that night.

There was more romance in my soul than Barbara Cartland could manage from the depths of her Chanel No 5 impregnated bloomers. Books have ruined my sex life too. No woman has ever taken me entirely seriously. Saying things like: "Do you realise that Sergeant Troy was based on a real person . . ." between thrusts, "his real name was . . . " does little for the establishment of a true person to person relationship. My person to person relationship consisted essentially of wanting everybody to be like people in books, especially girls. I am, I may say, unmarried.

Books have ruined my finances. I can earn countless amounts quite simply gadding about and getting stories and feeding it into newspapers and getting the editor to send me off to climes abroad and going on the television and radio more than I do. Somehow I can't put even the most meagre book down. I will read anything, from injunctions on the backs of Milk of Magnesia bottles written in three languages to the Vicar of Wakefield. I tell a lie: I jib at the Vicar of Wakefield.

My life has been ruined by books. I have even been forced to write them. There is no reason why I should not have earned a decent living ripping off folk by selling the buggers insurance policies they don't need, or designing high-rise flats you can't breathe in without causing dampness in the plaster-work, or even being a deputy editor on a newspaper. It was the incessant book-reading that made me do this most thankless of tasks for a living; writing for it. Ruined by reading I am. Just as well really. Can you imagine the ruin of me without books? And the ruin of you too?

The Arts

Lament for a dead king *16th Aug. 1978*

Within the last year a phenomenon has emerged in teenage culture. It may not appear as clearly as the punk rock phenomenon, but then it has been less assisted by a hungry media. It has been noted by schoolteachers and youth workers and discerning adults: it can be perceived simply by the chalked graffiti on walls and paving stones and by the legend carved on school desks. The legend simply says: 'Elvis the King Lives!'

It was a year ago today that Elvis Aaron Presley died in his Memphis mansion, where thousands will gather today to mourn their idol. Since his death, newspapers have produced the usual scandals – from stories by former sweethearts to his offer of assistance to the CIA – and a steady stream of his records on the radio ensures that Elvis isn't going to go away. And Elvis has been rediscovered by an audience too young to remember even the names of all the Beatles. They certainly couldn't know anything of the explosion in the world when Presley first emerged in 1956.

I was ll when I first heard him, and I had never heard music like it before. The roughness and the passion of it all was a fair cry from the Family Favourites stuff – Guy Mitchell and Doris Day and songs like *How Much Is that Doggie in the Window*. All sorts of other things began to change too. My elder brother was suddenly to be found wearing a black shirt and white tie, and his pal's drape jacket.

I couldn't understand what was happening. One minute my brother was a boy in baggy flannels who stayed in at night making crystal sets and reading the *Eagle*; the next he was a strange creature endlessly combing his hair back, only to finish the operation by messing it up at the front. I couldn't understand why my dad seemed so upset either; why he now referred to my brother as 'that bloody little spiv'.

I was fascinated by the glamour of the teenager: by the long greasy ducktail, the upturned collar, the low-slung hips, the slouch, the slur, the sneer. I used to spend my pocket-money in going down to the local cafe to play the juke box. Now I think about it, I must have looked strange in there – a wee boy in short trousers and good trim sitting on his own in that shabby little cafe playing the juke and watching the older kids.

For to me Elvis had style. He didn't seem like the showbiz I knew about. All the Americana I had been exposed to had consisted of sophisticated nightclub images like the Manhattan skyline on the Maxwell House coffee ads. Or Frank Sinatra with his tie undone. But Elvis wasn't like that at all, he growled and slurred and hollered his notes – 'Aint Nothing like a Hound-dog,' or 'Tutti-Frutti.'

The Presley explosion of 1956 is perhaps seen as rather an ingenious phenomenon now, and the post-Watergate nostalgia for the days of Ikeland innocence have led us to regard the rock 'n' roller with his leather jacket and DA hairstyle as redolent with charm. Witness the appeal of the TV series *Happy Days,* for instance.

But it was not always so. Way back in the mid-fifties, the original of all this, Elvis Presley, was seen as the swaggering embodiment of evil, and sensuality, and, yes, of miscegenation.

Rock 'n' roll did not create that younger generation: it merely came to be seen as its major expression. Since Presley, rock 'n' roll has grown to be the mainstream of popular music and culture, and its effects have passed into every area of society. Despite this, rock, and popular music in general, has been treated with some disdain by the organs of the cultural establishment.

The posh Sundays have their columns on 'Music', with other columns entitled 'Jazz' or 'Pop' pointing to a belief that the latter are – well – not quite 'Music'. The radio requires hushed Oxbridge voices for 'classical' music, as though the announcers are talking in church (and indeed they are in a way). The music syllabus in schools is surrealistically out of touch with the reality of today's music experience. We see instead the easy approval of those rather acquiescent youngsters who sing 'Land of Hope and Glory' at the dreary Proms concerts.

Even recently this virulent antagonism and snobbery to popular music was evinced when Glasgow's Apollo Theatre, the only venue in Scotland capable of showing the big rock stars, was closed by Mecca Ltd. A petition to save the theatre was organised and the signatures ran to 96,000. The Scottish Arts Council (who handed out £5.9 million last year) said, and I quote their spokesman: 'It is not the sort of thing into which we put money.'

Two hundred yards away stands the sort of thing into which the Scottish Arts Council put our money – the Scottish Opera Theatre. It cost a great deal of money to set up and it costs a great deal to run. As does the Scottish National Orchestra. I will not deny those organisations the right to an amount from the public purse, but there is some truth in the analysis that the majority pay for the arts which only an already wealthier minority enjoy. Certainly public antagonism to much of the policy of the Arts Council would be more easily assuaged if the same generosity in subsidising the traditional 'elite' arts was extended to what we might describe as the people's arts.

It is possible that Elvis Presley with his hips and his overt sexuality, and his position as a focus for a rebellious youth, had much to do with the continuing antagonism to rock 'n' roll, as he had much to do with its emergence and development. But were the classical music purists to place their ears a little closer to Presley's work, I think they might be surprised by the quality of it. For a start, besides his astonishing showmanship, Elvis did have a remarkable voice.

And a remarkable number of voices too. Among classically trained singers a multiplicity of voices tend to denote difficulty with shifts in register. In earlier days Elvis showed signs of strain in register transition, though this often expressed an affective innocence, and by 1959 he appears to have gained considerable control. He had always been able to duplicate the hoarse ecstatic sound of the R & B and Gospel singers, but it is in his ballads that you can hear the full-voiced high G and A's which an opera baritone might envy. And if anyone doubts that, just listen to the 1960 recording of 'It's Now Or Never' (an English version of 'O Sole Mio'), in which Presley ends on a full-voiced cadence of A-G-F that has all the power and style of a neopolitan tenor.

It is true in a way that Presley's early work was his most important, in the sense that his later records were built on his early vocal experiments, but though his fabled first album is a model of the freshness and vitality of rock and country music, Presley produced a late flowering of his art in the late sixties and early seventies, and we can see a truly remarkable number of classic recordings stretching throughout his career.

When I heard of the death of Elvis on August 16 last year, I hurried home, disbelieving, to find out if it could be true. It was true all right, and on the News they showed a clip from one of his early concerts, and I watched Elvis swivel his hips and I covered my face as the tears ran down. I suppose I remembered so many things through Elvis. Walking into cafes with my collar turned up, combing the grease through once thick hair, a time when, if I jived it was real, and not a stiff parody at a party.

I suddenly knew that I no longer had an older generation to mock at or despise, only colleagues more aged than myself. Soon I will have a younger generation to find fault with, if I don't have it already.

I remembered the wee boy in short trousers who once was me, sitting in that dingy little cafe, listening to 'Jailhouse Rock' on the juke a long time ago. All the slights and sneers of 20 years directed at popular music came back to me, and all the haughty arrogance of the 'music critics' and the Arts Councils in their dismissal of rock 'n' roll and Elvis Presley. And that night I wept for Elvis as he was when I first heard and imagined him. I wept for Elvis Presley, my dead king.

The kids who listen to his records today might get to hear a song from the film of 'Jailhouse Rock,' entitled 'You're So Young And Beautiful.' The last two lines in that song says what the kids are saying when they chalk 'Elvis the King Lives' on the pavement. It is a line which could well sum up Elvis Aaron Presley, who died, aged 42, a year ago today. It reads:

'And then you'll be forever young,
  and beautiful to me.'

And for millions around the world today, that's just what he is.

Artless Maggie

16th Aug. 1985

Here is another thing about Margaret Hilda Leaderene: she did not do Art at school, unless, that is, she was taught it by the jannie, during one of those milk breaks she once tried to get rid of. How else can you explain away the poor woman's taste? No qualified drawing master could ever have left a pupil with such a notion of architectural glory. I refer, of course, to that stately pile of brick-built vulgarity which Mrs T. and her hubby but recently chose when looking for a doss to spend their declining years in.

How deeply and appallingly apt it seems that their retirement home should be in a place called Dulwich. Nothing could more exemplify Mrs Thatcher's broad sweep of vision and her vibrant imagination than her decision to move into an estate. Oh, it is a highly exclusive estate, but it still sounds like a housing scheme to me. How apt it is that it should be a Barratt house as well.

Barratts have been in the forefront of providing new homes for new housebuyers, especially those who can be described as young couples. The nationwide firm build shiny new unpretentious homes, and good luck to them. Their advent into the upper bracket residences strikes one as a little like Marks and Sparks foray into men's suits – it'll be a decent suit, but it will not be Savile Row.

Oh, the house itself is no mere Nissen hut. It has got all the sorts of fancy security systems which, no doubt, ex-PMs need, and it has got a sauna and a garden with a lily pond and little wooden bridges to go with the little wooden heads, and three lavvies and everything. (Why, one wonders, do the better off seem to require so many latrines? Do they pee more than us?) The building is also very large and very, very expensive. None of the above makes it any the less dreary and predictable.

Mrs T. has, of course, been criticised for her choice of gaff. The architects were at her throat within minutes. Two chaps called David Nixon and Jan Kaplicky have but recently come up with a design for the sort of house they think our beloved Leaderene should be staying in, and endlessly going to the toilet in. Their suggested design is described thus: 'A lightweight geodetic box structure supported on four self-levelling legs,' and so on.

I saw a drawing of it. It looked like a machine for cutting chips. I noted also that the interior of this geodetic chipper was to be lined with 'a soft padded acoustic membrane.' As far as I can see, our two intrepid architects should be transported by their four self-levelling legs to just the sort of an establishment in which soft-padded interiors are an entirely traditional feature.

But the Thatcher's choice of house cannot help but give us an insight into the sheer banality of the PM's mind. A dreary big neo-Georgian edifice – a fake Georgian edifice at that – on a big estate with lots and lots of dreary neighbours just like yourself: there is no class in it at all. If I were to splash 400 grand on a big house I'd make sure it was a real Georgian house set in my own rolling acres with a porter's lodge half a mile away and liveried servants dodging about all over the joint. Dear God, the choices available to you for 400,000 spondulicks are damned near endless.

There is the castle on the shores of a Scottish loch, or the chateau on the Loire, or the Heathian flat in Albany, or the villa on the Cap d'Antibes, or the luxury penthouse in Chelsea or New York. I am damned sure I would not be moving the cut-moquette suite and onyx standard lamps into a fake house in an estate in Dullsville, sorry, Dulwich. A bit of style, my dears, a smidgeon of elegance and elan.

Your Urban Votaire cannot but admit to a slight gasp of astonishment when he first spied the photos of the Thatchers' frumpish acquisition. He could not help but think of perfectly decent houses which the Leaderette of the nation could have thought of buying for her old age. He – me that is – has coveted a few residences himself over the years.

I wanted to live in that building right across George Square from the City Chambers. I would have insisted in making my domicile out of the corner rooms at the top, the ones with great curved balconies. From there, I would survey the Square, making royal salutations to the populace below, the typists and clerks at lunchtimes, the hooligans waiting for the late buses at night. I would address the crowds on May Day. If I was an ex-Prime Minister I'd sort of like to keep my hand in.

I once wanted to live in the old Battlefield Mayfair cinema before it was ludicrously pulled down to make way for a hole in the road. I wanted to live in the empty vastness of it, like the Phantom of the Flicks occasionally showing the odd film or two to the pals. There is a particularly intriguing mansion I have long desired near me in a road I think called Hill Street. This magnificently sinister house has a glorious tower in it and looks like something out of 'Psycho.' I'd love it. The tower room at night, lit by candelabra, and myself cavorting about like something out of Edgar Alan Poe.

But the house for which I have yearned isn't really a house at all: it is only a room in it. I know I can write novels in this room. I can see myself entertaining in it, sipping old port while I casually play Mozart on the Bechstein. (In this room I can play the piano as well.) And what a breakfast an aristocrat like myself could have! In the library of Pollock House no less I would watch the sun steal across the dappled walls and look far away across my estate – a real estate, not the housing-scheme variety. I could be happy there.

But there you are, I am an aesthete at heart. It was easier for me than it was for Mrs T., of course: I did Art at school after all, and I would still be prepared to help her out with her education.

Beats to the Bar

10th July 1987

Harrison Birtwistle. There's a phrase for you. If it is a phrase. I looked it up and it is. It could even be called a musical phrase. According to the Oxford a musical phrase is: 'a short and more or less distinct passage of abour four bars.' If you have ever listened to the produce of Harrison Birtwhistle's febrile imagination you will suspect that Maestro Birtwistle has been in a lot more than four bars and has been drinking pints of absinthe in every one of them. Harrison Birtwistle's musical outpourings are a laugh.

Reference to a dictionary of music suggests that the chap is taken seriously. It says that his stuff is 'marked by genuine lyrical impulse built on dramatic use of ostinato and repeated thematic fragments.' It also says that 'a strong poetic feeling pervades all his work.' My view is that Harrison Birtwistle's compositions are about as poetic as a toilet seat. They are as lyrical as his own name. Mr. Birtwistle comes from Accrington. Poetic justice I call that.

I actually witnessed one of the said Accringtonian's works on the telly as it happens. There I was, just ready for the endeavours of a Saturday night, showered, shaved, and the other, slapping on the old Antaeus after-shave and plumping the breast-pocket hanky and on came the Harrison Birtwhistle. It was great. How I did laugh. I spent an hour and a half in fascinated horror as this 'opera' slid across the cathode ray tube and my amazed eyes. The opera was about Punch and Judy.

I ever thought Punch and Judy rather strange and in fact rather surreal and I suspect that the bold Harrison had much the same notion but Punch and Judy was positively the Critique of Pure Bloody Reason in comparison to what the lad from Accrington (I keep bringing that burg in: Accrington is even dafter a name than Birtwhistle), was capable of dreaming up as music. You should have seen the opera.

Punch was played by a bloke wearing torn yellow tights, a half-shaved head with hair dyed white and green, white face, and a bemused expression. Considering what the poor fellow was obliged to sing I am not surprised at the bemused expression. I am astonished at what opera singers will do for money, that's all.

Judy was clad in a white party dress and was required to screech at a level consistent with a sexual assault. The rest of the cast clearly had difficulty in following the harmonies which is to say that even the most tone deaf in the land could have sung more in tune.

It would appear that Mr. Birtwistle is highly regarded for this ability to produce the sound of the asylum. I am a shocking Philistine for drawing this matter to your attention. If what I said last week in this blatt is true, (I said that critics were in the business of writing fashion notes for New Emperors), then it is doubly true for modern composers.

It is my view that modern composers are at it. Modern composers, modern music critics, modern almost anything, have a knack of telling you that you are nothing but a middle-brow, because you require a plot in a book, tune in song, or a bit of sense in a picture.

In sheer physical terms I am undeniably a high-brow, even with the cover up hairstyle. Metaphorically I am not even a gutter-brow: I am practically subterranean. I do not understand what is called modern music. I do not understand it at all.

I never grasped the lyrical delights in Benjamin Britten. I always thought Peter Pears a dreadful old queen who couldn't even croon, though I accepted that this might have been due to his chum's appalling music.

I reckon I can play the piano better than Peter Maxwell Davies and as all I can play is a spirited rendition of Schuman's traumerei and half of Bonny Mary of Argyle that says little for Pete's prowess. Hour after hour and day after day sees the Third Programme 'educating' us all in the matter of modern symphonic suppurations. People PAY to go to such concerts. It is all a great mistake. Here is what I am going to do.

I am going to issue a challenge to Michael Tumelty of this blatt, (incidentally do you not think 'Tumelty' a wonderful name for a music critic – 'Tumelty, tumelty-tum-te-tum, tumulty-tum-te-tum-tum' is just right for the Archers theme tune), a challenge to our own Mick. The challenge is this: defend it all. Tell us how Maxwell, Britten, and, not least,

Birtwhistle, are real musicians while Chuck Berry, Jerry Lee Lewis, Elvis, and James Last, are not. Okay, I will leave out James Last.

I want Mr. Tumelty to make out a case for Harrison Birtwhistle's splendid use of ostinato (it means 'obstinate' or 'persistent'). A case for Charles Ives use of 'clusters' – this means rattling your forearm at random across the piano keyboard. Should Mr. Tumelty come up with a reason why the splendid music of, say, Eric Coates, is considered inferior by the 'serious' music critics to that of any of the people named above I shall even buy him a drink. It is time for we Philistines to rise.

Film Fun   *15th July 1988*

Every now and again, like everybody else, your Urban V, finds himself exhausted by his labours down the boozer and ready and waiting to sit in front of the idiot box till he falls asleep, which is generally within the space of three minutes or about enough time for Joan Collins to change into eight separate costumes which is all you get to see these days on television, but even more occasionally up jumps a movie which has got film stars and scenery and plots and, in fact, you end up riveted to the old cathode-ray tube.

It reminds you of going to the movies when you were a boy and the movies made sense. Do you remember those days? Back then you could even re-tell the story to your pals. It was a long time back but. These days films are Art. This means that nobody understands a minute of them but you are damned if anybody finds you out in your ignorance. There is, however, film fun in today's cinema.

There are times, in fact, when fun goes over the top. Times indeed when the contemporary film became so wonderful that it isn't possible to take the piss out of the pretentiousness because it does that for you already. Let us take a recent production. You can see this, if youse want, in London's Rupert Street. (That is a dead giveaway – Rupert Street forsooth: where all the Ruperts go.) It stars chaps and chapettes with international names like 'Jim Van Der Woude' and 'Stephane Excoffier.' Directors of photography include stout fells such as Theo Van De Sande and Goert Giltaij. It was produced and directed by Mr Jos Stelling.

When I was a mere lad I could tell what kind of movie that was, just by the names. They showed it at the Grand Central and frustrated elderly blokes made furtive movements beneath their gaberdine coats while a row of adolescent boys laughed coarsely for 10 minutes before they were put out. This movie doesn't even have the benefit of fulfilling whatever needs such cineastes of the past required. This film is called The Pointsman and it is Art incarnate. It is a right good laugh.

Wait till you hear the synopsis. It has a dimension pertinent to our land. 'Accidentally stepping off a train in the remote Scottish Highlands,' says this blurb, 'a chic Frenchwoman...' I love it already, A.J. I love it... 'finds herself stranded with a Dutch railway points-operator who leads a lonely, basic existence.' Well he would, wouldn't he? It's the remote Scottish Highlands after all. Even the bloody Highlanders lead a lonely, basic existence up there. What would you expect if you were a Dutch railway-points operator? Breakfast at Tiffany's and dinner on Ari's yacht? It goes on sublimely.

'Lacking a common language, they' (the chic Frenchwoman and the thick Dutch railway chap), 'build up a network of gestures and expressions...' This is just as well because I am going to find trouble with the chic French language let alone the sheer romance of Dutch railwayspeak, 'the woman wears her most provocative clothes to tease never-felt emotions from her virgin' (sic) 'acquaintance until jealousy, desire, and frustration consume him.' So far so good. A.J., but when does she get to take her knickers off? It's not that kind of movie, Bob. Just wait till ya hear the end...

'Enthralling performances generate a claustrophobic tension that seethes into every cranny of a painstakingly detailed single set...' Wait there, A.J., wait there: I geddit, I geddit.

I do too. I get it all right. I've had it, what's worse, and I've had it up to here, pal. I KNOW this movie. There is only one set and it made out of emulsioned hardboard and wishful thinking. The actors are made out of balsa wood, the plot out of desperation, and the dialogue out of the asylum. Do not worry, little ones. You will yet be able to enjoy this absurdity along with your Gitanes fags and coffee and croissants. The blurb takes care of that: it explains the simple lack of sense and plot.

'Taking no account of plausibility, the film's exploration of the uses and abuses of power...' Dear Heaven: I remember when the only exploration in the movies was when Big John Wayne was looking for Chief Scar or Stewart Granger was hunting big animals to shoot between their ravening eyes. I simply ADORE the phrase 'Taking no account of plausibility, Mr. Kemp, I am looking for £300,000 a year plus exxes.' There is a lassie I fancy in Babbity Bowsters. 'Taking no account of plausibility, Lorna...' I shall say. This is what Art is all about and I am glad of it.

I have seen the poster for this film. It looks as if it was directed by Edvard Munch. An absolute scream, in fact, my dears. A critic says it is 'worthy and enjoyable' which is much the same as inverting it. Anybody with half a brain, except maybe a film critic, knows that it is specious, valueless, suicidally boring and would make an afternoon spent in Bellshill Industrial Museum (if such exists and I will bet it will if it doesn't yet), look, well, plausible.

In the meantime another giant of the cinema, a Mr Ingrid... sorry, Ingmar, Bergman, is to celebrate his birthday in the 'wild wastelands of Sweden.' I think it rather a pity that he didn't celebrate the past 30 years there and given us all a break. I don't know how many hours I have spent in Mr. Cosmo's fleapit back in the old days coughing blood after 80 French fags and spending the week's wages on bags of Raspberry Ruffles watching silly films neither I nor the object of my less than intellectual desire could understand so that I could get the lassie to take no account WHATSOEVER of a plausibility. In a way I am glad I am no longer as young and attractive as once I was. Now I get to see real films. Ones with plots I can tell you about afterwards.

Dirty words   *5th Jan. 1990*

Book at bedtime? That'll be right. At bedtime you are looking for the mug of Horlicks and a detective story by some abject snob like Marjory Allingham. What you are not looking for is a dose of carnality, unless, that is, you have somebody else in your bed, in which case you are hardly likely to be reading books or listening to anything else other than heavy breathing. Radio 4 has other ideas though.

Before that glorious wee tune that ends your night for you – Sailing By, I think its called – you are currently getting Mr. David Herbert Lawrence's novel *Lady Chatterley's Lover*. God knows what ideas the book at bedtime is putting into the virtuous heads of spinster ladies in Tunbridge Wells and the like. It must be pretty traumatic for whores in Perth, let alone spinsters in Tunbridge Wells. Are there whores in Perth? Are there virtuous ladies in Tunbridge whatsit? Not after hearing all that sex on Radio 4 there won't be.

The trial over the book was re-enacted on the same radio station at the beginning of the week and I listened to it. Said the Beeb's announcer just before the programme: 'Some listeners may be offended by the language used in this broadcast...' I will guarantee that some listeners were, myself included, oddly enough. I am not used to switching on the radio to hear chaps talking like myself unless it is myself. Sure, I don't mind swearie-words. As the young 20-year-old lassie who was one of the witnesses for the defence during the trial said herself, I know all the Anglo-Saxonisms. A book at bedtime might just not be the place for them though, and cetainly not the time. It is not the words which upset though. It's the book.

Now, as it happens, the august deputy editor of this blatt thinks that *Lady Chatterley's Lover* is a grand book. He says it is one of the best books Lawrence wrote. He says it is beautiful. He says it is moving. I say it is rubbish, and filthy rubbish at that. Mellors indeed! Chap's simply not a gentleman. Not that this matters really. Neither was Lawrence. In fact, as far as I can see, Lawrence wasn't only not a gentleman, he wasn't much of a man at all. Bloody mammy's boy if you ask me.

His da' in *Sons And Lovers* should have given him a good drubbing and a backhander to the boy's mum to boot. Mellors seems to me to be the sort of wimp who is always sniffing round birds but can't buy his round down the boozer. As for his language to his lady love: in all my years I have never used such filth to a wummin, and certainly not in bed with her. Women have sometimes used them regarding my performance, but no' me. I keep a civil tongue in my head.

On the other hand I wouldn't go about banning books or whatever. I haven't the slightest objection to my servants reading rubbish like *Lady Chatterley's Lover*. Or even *Last Exit To Brooklyn*, which I note has just been made into a film. Our deputy editor isn't alone in his arcane tastes. Anthony Burgess, no less, says the Last Exit book was moving as well. He also described it as 'gritty', as in 'gritty realism'. I know – you know – what gritty realism is. It is foulmouthed and unpleasant. Unpleasant is the word.

As I set before this keyboard thing I see pinned on it a slip of paper which states: 'Dear shop-keeper. As one of your regular customers I object to the sale of pornography at this shop'. I don't know why the chap I sometimes share this terminal with ha such a legend on his keyboard. I don't know why he objects really to pornography. It is not because D.H. Lawrence's appalling novel is pornography – and I do not think it is – that I object to it. It is because it is rotten. Equally, *Last Exit To Brooklyn* is a filthy book about disgusting things and people, but I can cope with that. Quite simply, though, it, like the Lady Chatterley book, is both boring and demeaning. And a touch less than erotic.

Erotic is grand. Erotic I like. One of the reasons why I have never been able to grasp why some feminists object so strongly to soft porn – more often than not actually erotica – is because I suspect that most sensible people rather like it, and erotica is to do with, after all, the human condition, or at least the condition which humans get into from time to time. Hard-core porn is different and makes you feel unclean even as it might arouse the flesh. *Lady Chatterley's Lover* is not pornography in the sexual sense, but it seems to me to be a dispiriting novel. Curiously dated as well. Old-fashioned, sort of. Dirty words.

Some of the nicest words are dirty words though. And it is difficult to get annoyed about their use, especially with a bit of imagination and good humour behind it. The current book at bedtime strikes me as a dose of Harold Robbins with a touch more smaltz even. Daft. Nearly as daft as prosecuting it. But not as daft as having it before bed. Ruins the Horlicks. And, probably, your love-making as well, if you should be so lucky.

The Big Man?   *12th Jan. 1990*

Maurice may dear, didn't I draw blood? What a gloriously orotund letter you contributed the other day, complaining about my tedious arrogance. Why, you old charlatan, you old sychophant, you damn-near had me laughing and that would never do for a sardonic fellow like myself. Less sardonic fellows who remember your varied career in the Scottish Establishment – you really should take a wee squint at the pomposity of your entry in the Scottish Who's Who – were laughing fit to burst. Chris Grieve has had an epileptic fit in his burial mound. That'll see you off, old man, and don't bother replying. Sue me.

Most of you don't even know for a minute who I am talking about. You are all the better for it. Maurice is one of those chaps who set us all up for being Scottish into the second half of the twentieth century. Jings, now, what a stushie at the Mains it has all turned out to be. Considering how august the entire division of pisspots who were intent on bringing us all into the second half of the etc. were, it is hardly surprising just how abject the second half in Scotland has turned out. I will give you another luminary.

Willie McIlvanney is just that. What a fine-looking man William is! Not a kick off Rabbie Burns. The weemenfolk on the telly have horrible hots for him and the poofs on the same, well, organ, are not averse to the timeless Kilmarnockian profile. Willie has got the sort of grainy Ayrshire voice which English idjits take for integrity. He writes books as well.

As it happens I think, for what that's worth, that he has written a couple of very fine books indeed, and I believe that *Docherty* and *A Gift From Nessus* are the sort of novels which could have made a start to a career not far removed from a D. H. Lawrence, about whom I had words to say the other week. David Herbert wrote, among some masterpieces – *The Lost Girl, The Rainbow,* and *Kangaroo* come to mind – a dreadful amount of drivel. McIlvanney is a fine sonsie fellow with a fine and timeless Ayrshire profile but he should have been persuaded not to indulge in notions of the big city. The Big City now.

Mr McIlvanney came to the Big City with a big Kilmarnock bunnet and took one look at the lights and decided that this was the Big Time. Boays like myself were brought up here and thought Paris or London or New York was. It was a big Kilmarnock bunnet all the same and William has had one side of it covering one eye, and sometimes both eyes, for over 30 years. Willie is not the only one who has lowered the bunnet over the brow, and looked at the shadow of the skip. You should have seen the drivel some chap on our sister paper came out with the other day.

Ach, it wasn't just *The Evening Times,* McIlvanney was on the TV set the other day along with other worthies, talking mince. These media chaps, when they want to go about speaking of the Glasgow renaissance, go about giving every hour of tape to everybody they ever met in the Abbotsford Bar, Edinburgh or the Lamb and Flag, London. I seen it. Muriel Gray has become the sort of person about whom you could genuinely give a line concerning tedious arrogance and maybe even Maurice of the cravat would get away with that. Also, she is reading form the sort of bleary-eyed script I was writing myself years back. Billy Connolly is simply too good for that kind of crap, but out of decency gives the occasional interview. If I see another professional Glaswegian on the box I shall simply scream, my dears, I shall.

Let me give you another professional Glaswegian. Stand up, Mr William "Toe" Elliot. Mr Elliot is currently a prisoner in the Barlinnie Prison. Mr Elliot, for whatever reason best known to my editors on this very blatt, was but recently acknowledged talking obscenities in some sort of debate in the Special Unit – where else – and in this and other newspapers, Mr Elliot, if you didn't know is a murderer who was finally put away for stabbing one of his (homosexual) drug dealers up the anus with a boning knife. The young man died in seconds, bleeding though his bowels. Mr Elliot gets visits from arty chaps and chapettes, which is more than the poor sods doing time for non-payment of fines ever get.

What has this got to do with anything? I will tell you. McIlvanney based one of his characters in the book which is now being filmed – *The Hard Man* – on a well-known Glasgow thug, whom McIlvanney found romantic. The same thug once worked alongside the same William "Toe" Elliot. Damon Runyon often pronounced upon this very curious notion of romanticism. I remember the thug upon whom McIlvanney based his creation and I find it pretty hard to take.

You will pardon my sudden burst of unctuous disapproval. I was brought up where he was. Not Kilmarnock, like Willie, Not the splendid clubs of the Scottish Establishment, as Maurice of the cravat was. Here. God rot it.

Graffiti   *22nd Dec. 1989*

Indeed, sir, it is a sad day. Wrote a reader, a Mr Stephen J. Newton, of Callander: "It is indeed a sad day . . ." I will tell Mr Newton and the rest of youse out there and you are as well keeping it in mind: there are a lot of sad days in the year, the

25th of December being foremost among them if you ask me. But Mr Newton had a point at that. Incensed he was at the fact that two absolute bananas who had been found guilty of defacing public property, to wit, a bridge and to wit, by painting slogans about how none of us should pay the poll tax and instead not bother paying any money at all for removing graffiti. This is beginning to get confusing. One of the vandals was a schoolteacher. I am not surprised. it was only a matter of time that the dominies would get infected by the scum they are standing in front of day in day out.

Mr Newton's grip seems reasonable. The total fines which the two over-educated miscreants incurred did not meet even half the cost of removal of the slogans. I may say that I am distressed about the slogans one finds painted up in every dod of masonry on the Lomondside road, mainly by demented Nationalists. Arab nationalists it would seem too. But then the courts have got it all wrong no doubt, along with the rest of us.

Graffiti is probably now called community art. Once as an art teacher I set the weans to work in drawing out a brick wall on the basis that bricks were what the brats were as thick as. The last bit of this so-called lesson was getting the homunculi to scribble rubbish all over it. "Sharon loves Gaz"; "FTP 1690"; "Young Tory Toi Rule". One of my favourite pieces of racist graffiti was the one prominently displayed on a wall of a South-side Glasgow school which reads as follows: "Nigers out!" Why they picked on Nigerians and not, for instance, the denizens of Tanzania or Zimbabwe is beyond me.

Anyway, the children set to their task with zeal. Every spiky-haired little creature measured, ruled, drew, painted, and in every way exerted their aesthetic on the paper with a view to completing the wall just for the chance to scrawl a variety of obscenities over it. Except for two wee girls in the class. Sharon Biggam and Lesley Roberts refused point-blank to deface their walls. I may even have threatened them with severe beatings with the super-heavy Lochgelly which, in time-honoured fashion, I kept permanently within the sleeves of my blackstuff gown. To no avail. Steadfastly the two wee girls, who are not wee any more at all, refused to act in such a wanton way. It made you think there was still hope for the world. A dreadful little snotter of a boy called Young was lovingly inscribing his painting with a description of myself which had a reference to male genitalia.

But it is not just graffiti which is all right. So is anything. How about those Barlinnie chaps who, because they had attended some ridiculous set of lectures by sensitive souls determined on the reform of the criminal classes, were permitted to have their sweethearts and children in to see them for a Christmas party. One of the felons dressed up as Santa Claus. A grand time was had by all.

Probably the Special Unit have had an even better wee celebration and the inmates, sorry, patrons, were served pressed duck with all the trimmings by Lord Mackay of Clashfern with an after-dinner concert by Luciano Pavarotti and Dame Kiri thingmy. A variety houris – I said houris – will have been brought in from the BBC Club, all of them with psychology degrees and distinguished dads, to peel grapes for the bastards as they lolled insouciantly on Louis Quatorze divans smoking hashish from handcrafted Edinburgh crystal hookahs. I will bet you that it is not a kick in the bahookie off the above scenerario in all reality.

As it happens, your Urban Voltaire's heart softens a little at this time of year. I have no objection at all to Christmas parties in the nick and wives and sweethearts being there too. I should have thought it only reasonable, though, that everybody inside got a chance at the same, and not just those bloody chancers in the Special Unit or doing their O-grades in mailbag technology. I should have thought too that it would be somewhat more reasonable if the prisoners who are, after all, locked up because they are bad persons, were occasionally to be told how bad they are instead of getting a collection of female journalists misty-bloody-eyed about what a hard life they are having.

I should have thought that the two halfwits whose politics

behoved them to scrawl mince over walls should have got a dose of the jail without the Christmas party and a swift skelp with a sjambok just to learn them. That's the kind of boay am urr. I'll show you Christmas and goodwill to men. I said this to Big Rad the barman. Rad is a graduate of the University of Life and a grand teacher to boot in the ways of the world. I asked the man if he agreed with my grandly bilious viewpoint. "Ach, it's Christmas," he said, "here's a half and all the best."

Travels

London Revisited *9th Sept. 1987*

I went to London early in '64 having by then exhausted the sophisticated bohemianism of the West End of Glasgow. Thousands of young idjits did likewise. We had sat listening to the second Stones album long enough and wanted the real thing. No matter how many white-painted rooms with Japanese lamp-shades and casual mattresses on the floor that you sat and smoked an illicit joint on, it wasn't enough. London beckoned. The streets were paved with celebrities.

Nobody who was anybody lived in Glasgow. That year, in fact, nobody who was anybody lived anywhere at all except London. So, like every other nobody, I went down to London to seek my fortune, or anyway to get to wear dark glasses in Greek Street with all the other celebs. Once I got to be one myself that was.

My first day in London. It was, I remember, a bright retina-smarting morning when I woke up. The night before I'd arrived late at the place which my elder brother shared with another bloke and three girls. That had a smart London air about it too, but the night before I had been too exhausted and, I suppose, excited to notice anything about my surroundings except that a former tenant had left several sculptures of his own designing. They were made out of bits of car doors and I inwardly knew they were appalling, but this was London: what the hell did I know?

The morning was bright and fresh and washed, the way London always is first thing on a summer's day. I could feel the exhilaration, like something out of a toothpaste ad. 'This is London!' I cried to my brother in glee. 'This is London,' repeated my brother in a sepulchral voice, 'The King is dead!' We laughed hysterically. It was very heaven to be alive.

This was just outside Sandwell Mansions, a large red-brick and stucco tenement in West Hampstead. We passed the Railway Tavern where, I was told, Diz Disley played at weekends. The other Diz – Gillespie – had played there last month. I insisted we had a pint of bitter in this legendary juke-joint which I had only heard of a minute before. The beer was awful: I drank it like nectar.

Like all the thousands of young provincial searchers after the big time the first move was to sign on. This I did in a large dusty building in Marylebone. I remembered Marylebone because it was on the Monopoly board. For a good few months lots of district names brought that Monopoly board to mind. Remember this too: I always lost at Monopoly, I always went broke. The real Monopoly board of the Great Wren brought me to the same situation, only this time it was to prove real money. I went broke.

For the next three years I was to be broke all the time, chronically, despairingly broke. When social workers tell you that some family is on the poverty line because the weans can't get a new BMX bike, I have to laugh about the poverty line because I was on it, and below, off and on right throughout my sojourn in the Smoke.

I never told anyone when I hitch-hiked back up north. I let them know that I was practically the bloody mayor of the entire burg. I didn't tell them about the scraping up the rent for the housing agency which was run by a six-foot-high West Indian who wore a black beret and shades and who was called Mr Ulysses. Or the model lodging houses, or their London equivalents. The dossing down on friends' floors till they insisted on my disappearance. The frightened shop-lifting in Sainsbury's in Kilburn High Road because I hadn't actually eaten for two days. The lousy wages for wee unskilled Scottish guys whom the Cockneys called 'Jock,' and made it sound as if you were being called a Tartan nigger. I didn't tell anyone about that. I lied instead.

For most of the time I lived in Kilburn, in a disgusting flat, made infinitely more appalling by myself and the other lads, all of whom were Scottish or Irish, for we made virtually no English friends. No. 45 Cavendish Road it was, a few doors up, I was to discover many years later, from the house in which the mass-killer Dennis Nielsen was already burying his victims. Kilburn was that sort of place, and it still looks it.

Kilburn was the big Irish area of London and the Kilburn High Road was packed full of Irish boozers in which big red-faced paddies with long sideburns listened lacrymosely to songs on the juke box such as Paddy Reilly singing The Town I Loved So Well. On my trip down memory lane I nipped into one of the most famous of such establishments, Biddy Mulligan's.

Paddy Reilly was still rattling away on the juke, and everybody still drank Jameson's. The men had sideburns and red faces, and there were the very same young sad colleens sitting there in their fading finery still looking for work better paid than charring. I visited the North London Tavern, scene of the fight which my pal Gerry Thomas had unwisely started and in which I saw in real life what is never off the movies – a bloke being punched through a window. It is a lot more devastating in real life, I can tell you.

The old Kilburn State Cinema, which once housed one of Europe's finest cinema organs, is now a closed-down Bingo Hall, and the Old Prague restaurant where Tony did the best steak marsala I ever tasted for six bob is now a ubiquitous Indian restaurant. I even visited, out of a queer feeling of emotional necessity rather than nostalgia, 45 Cavendish Road. It was being renovated by a firm of gentrifiers.

But Kilburn was low-life when I lived in it; it was no place for dreamers like myself to meet the pop stars and the big guys in advertising, or the TV, or the journalism, or anything glamorous at all. For that you had to go to Hampstead, district then of all the intelligentsia and all the mountebanks who created Swinging London.

I once saw Paul McCartney in a coffee bar in Hampstead. Another time I stood at a bar counter just beside the critic Kenneth Tynan. He had a lazy drawl with an excited stutter in the middle of it. That was in a bar called The Flask. Nothing would do but a whizz round all the pubs I remembered in Hampstead and I went first to where my meeting with Tynan, which as far as I know went unrecorded by the critic, had taken place these years ago.

There was an air of gloom about the bar, although it still looked pleasant enough. A Scots barman called Dave from Kilmarnock told me the reason for the gloom. The family who had been tenants of the place for 51 years were being turned out and replaced by managers.

This is a system increasingly used by the big brewers in London and a foolish idea I think too. Mind you, the Scottish barman called Dave wouldn't serve a whisky later on that night because he had put the clock on five minutes fast and had rung the last bell. Maybe managers aren't such a bad idea after all.

The famed Jack Straw's Castle hadn't changed in any way at all except one: it is now greatly favoured by the gay community. Back when I went there it was violently hetero and I didn't do so bad myself.

I made brief visits to the other local pubs I once went to in search of famous intellectuals. Spaniard's Inn still looks like a set for a Gainsborough costume drama film but the Old White Bear has been extensively refurbished. It is, oddly enough, owned by one of our own, Glen... who also owns Smith's Bar in West Nile Street. Trust a pub owned by a Scotsman to be the venue to get your cashmere jacket stolen by a customer, and I did. I'll bet the thief was also from north of the border.

But 20 years ago or so I could ill afford pubs, especially in Hampstead, which is, incidentally, remarkably unchanged. It is unchanged quite simply because it was a wealthy suburb then, and it is even wealthier now; even semi-detached houses are in the half-million quid class. This time around I could afford a few whiskies, but it was still a business of pressing your proletarian nose against the window pane.

I decided on one more trip down memory lane – I decided to visit the old sweat shop where I once laboured. A rundown building it had been. It was more than rundown when I saw it after an absence of all those years. With a glorious irony I was there just in time to see it being demolished. Someone had set it on fire the week before. It wisnae me, and I have an alibi, but it brought gladness to my heart.

Bordering on the ridiculous 14th Sept. 1988

The Borders has been an anomaly in the history of the past two and a half centuries of Scotland. Not the Highlands with its romance, kilts, and poverty, or the Central Lowlands and its own special grandeur, from slums to mercantile splendour. But here we are in Scotland all the same – why else would the Borderers have fought so much? A cause like a country could be the only reason.

The Borders to me summoned up visions of complacency and rich farmers. To a Glaswegian it makes little difference whether it is north or south; outside the Magic City they are all teuchters to me. Peebles was the first stop.

Peebles is widely held to be not quite the Borders, although it is: it is the first town you encounter after the signpost. Peebles is not quite the Borders because it is too nice, too pleasant, too twee perhaps, to belong to what, I was to discover, was a depressed region.

In Peebles there are lots of. anglified accents among the locals, let alone visitors. The Peebles Hydro is vast, magnificent, expensive. The huntin', fishin', shootin' boys go there. The High Street is packed with discreet little shops for wealthy, rather stupid, aristos to make desultory purchases. If the Royals hadn't discovered Ballater, they would have settled in Peebles.

It is a handsome town with fine grey stone buildings, though I discovered hidden tensions in the place all the same. The board giving details of all the nearby places of interest had graffiti on it from some local malcontent. Beside the bold blandishment for mansions and beauty spots, someone had chalked up on the board as a place of interest 'The Dole.'

Peebles doesn't look though anybody is employed: it looks as though everybody employed somebody else. Rogerson's shoe

135

shop has Church's shoes cheaper than you can get them in Glasgow. The reason, I was told, was that everybody can afford the £90 or so that such brogans cost in this little burg. The Tontine Hotel was full of old chaps in very clean raincoats. You live longer here and you can afford it too.

In the oldest, most old-fashioned, newsagents I have seen in 20 years, an old crone is positively shouting at the customers, resentful of their existence, let alone their presence. She is the angriest wee woman I have ever seen. The lady customers, in their tweed skirts and sensible shoes, mutter 'Well I never' in Oxbridge tones, but are unsure about how to deal with such proletarian rudeness.Tourists queue up to buy maps, bars of Ritter Sports chocolate, and David Steel's book on the area. The entire High Street is lined with well-kept little shops or solicitors' offices. In Peebles the lawyers still call themselves 'Writers' in keeping with old tradition.

There is a limit to tradition, however, for the County Hotel has punk barmaids who are surprisingly courteous. And in the Green Trees Hotel – which I last visited during the Police Federation annual bash – you are confronted with the Peebles population which isn't the county set. It turns out to be a trades holiday and the lads are in there, swearing gaily, and rattling back lager.

Outside of my city, Glasgow, you find the two nations: outside of Glasgow the lower orders cling to their class difference. It is, sometimes, an attractive trait among the Scots.

Get yourselves to Selkirk some time. It is the strangest town in Scotland. As we passed through I discovered another angry denizen. If I thought the aged lady in the Peebles newsagent was fired with ire, dear God, she was saintly in comparison to the traffic warden who directed the cars at Selkirk Cross. 'Bastard!' he was shouting at some transgressor. I cannot tell you what he called me. A dreadfully short-tempered people, the borderers are.

In Selkirk the populace are short-tempered, depressed, happy, and friendly; all in the one. This town is aff its heid.

David Palmer's butcher's shop is emblazoned with the legend 'The Scottish Haggis Making Champion' across the length of it. In an upstairs window a large Alsatian sits, yawning. It'd be a bit less unconcerned if it knew what made a champion haggis, I thought.

But then, everything is crazy in Selkirk. Another shop advertises 'The Selkirk Bannock.' The Selkirk Bannock turns out to be a bun. There is a quite wonderful sign in the Ming Chun Chinese Takeaway. 'Take Away Chinese Food' it reads, and underneath, 'Sorry, no dogs.' Selkirk Sheriff Court is an august building which has a shoe shop inculcated in it just beside its Georgian portico, and 'Ye Olde Court House Coffee Shoppe' on the other side. Nothing makes sense in Selkirk.

Almost as if to prove my point, a well-spoken old man in a grand tweed suit passes by, staggering with a controlled drunken lurch. 'F... cheek' he says to me beerily but with a chuckle in his throat. 'Bloody girl put me out,' he said. 'Of course, I'v had enough,' he slurred. 'Don't need a bloody girl to tell me that.' The elderly, clearly middle-class, gent swayed aristocratically up the road chuckling and shouting 'F... cheek' at volume. In the Cross Keys bar there was a Durex machine which bore the legend 'By R.C. Products.' I told you Selkirk was off its head.

In the lovely little Town Arms Inn there were two water taps, the one claiming to be Ettrick water, the other water from the River Yarrow. One side was for Tories, the other for Labour. It was the noisiest pub I have ever been in. Selkirk would make a fine setting for a hatter and a dormouse.

By now at least a few of you chaps out there must be recognising that my sojourn round Scotland could be subtitled a trip round the various boozers. But what's wrong with that?

People are the way they are because of the way they get on with each other, and they do that in public places. There is a wee village in the Borders called Brigham, for instance: the Fisherman's Arms it is called and the insurance salesman whom I met there surfaced in yet another Cross Keys bar, this

time a hotel. And in Kelso at that. In the Whipman Bar (sic),
late at night, there are a plethora of young men and women
shouting as raucously as you will find in the middle of the
Gallowgate. A sign on the wall reads: 'Anyone, male or female,
caught fighting or dumping property in these premises will be
reported to the police OR BANNED FOR EVER.'

This is a far cry from the way I imagined Kelso – and a
zillion years away from the splendid hotel in which myself and
my entourage are staying. The Sunlaws House Hotel is owned
by the Duke and Duchess of Roxburghe. I don't know if you
have seen the Duchess herself, but she is a definite stoatir:
sorry to drop into Mollyweirese.

The hotel, it turns out, is the only joint with style in the
entire region. It is a damned good diner and, so far on my
journey through this benighted land, the only place with any
imagination. I am told that the Duchess is behind all this
splendour. If Scottish tourism is to work at all, then we are
needing a pretty peeress like herself to show us all off.

Kelso is, I was to find, a strangely characterless town. The
locals sport the same Vyella Tattersall check shirts and green
wellies and tweed pudding basin hats as I saw in Peebles, but
with a less confident air. A wonderful cinema in peeling stucco
called The Roxy lies forlorn and empty looking when it should
be asking for a National Trust grant. A young man, sturdy as a
farmer's boy, is wearing girls' lacy gloves and a pink and green
mohican above his bucolic features. The town square at first
looks spacious and prosperous. On closer investigation it is
tatty and floored in litter. Shops selling spurious tartan
artefacts abound. There is little sign of the Borders' most
famous products, textiles and knitwear.

If I thought Kelso was bad, it was a bigger shock to
encounter Hawick.

Hawick: you think of rugby, and of cashmere, and of a
certain douce prosperity. You would be wrong. Hawick has a
long main street in which there are buildings which should be
interesting but have had dullness of mind applied to them. The

Hawick town hall is a decent-sized edifice somewhat reminiscent of Rutherglen's towered equivalent. The doors are dusty and weathered, and the building itself gloomy with neglect. A noticeboard in one of its windows heralds all the glorious things the tourist and resident can get up to. The notice has been clipped out of a brochure and clearly assembled by a primary school child who had finished his sums earlier than his classmates. It is faded with the sun of years.

A little farther on I came to The Tower Hotel. A plaque announces that the building contains the old Black Tower of the Douglas family. The entire structure, hotel and all, has been allowed to fall apart and what should have been an historical landmark is now a disused bricked-up model lodging house. A nearby pub is named after me. 'Jack's Bar' is dilapidated and raucous-looking at the same time.

East German style industrial estates ring the town and lie cheek by jowl with the famed Hawick rugby ground. Not an impressive sight. As elsewhere in the border towns there are equestrian statues intended to mark the Ridings, that inexplicable Border pastime, but little thought has gone into the surrounding planning. The statuary was festooned in wrappers from a nearby chip shop.

There is a deal of unemployment about in the Borders and the mills, no longer provide rich livings, if they ever did. This comes as rather a shock to myself. Certainly the small town of Melrose is more, as I had imagined, a Borders town. It is a rich little place with lots of rich little people. Smart little shops from bakers to drapers. It's a place with only one claim to fame, Melrose Abbey.

As the proverbial every schoolboy knows this is the legendary spot where Robert the Bruce's heart, returned from the Holy Land, was buried at High Altar. Where one of the windows is commemorated by Sir Walter Scott's *Lay of the Last Minstrel.* Where generations of English kings exercised frequent arson. It is historic. It is famous. It is, in fact, a collection of bits of old stone and they make you pay a quid to go through a turnstile and look at the rubble.

More Bedside Urban Voltaire

Needless to say, there were droves of tourists with Sheffield accents taking snapshots. I note that the tourists also purchase postcards of the ruin. Tourists indulge in the process of duplication everywhere though: I don't know why. We go back into the little town and attempt to buy glasses of beer in a very smart hotel but are turned away and directed towards a tea shoppe. If ruins don't depress you, beerless hotels would.

But at least Melrose possessed a quiet, middle class, moneyed confidence to it. You should see Galashiels. It is a town which would make Shotts look effervescent. Unlike other towns in this region Galashiels has no pretension to uniqueness and has clearly set its cap at High Street merchandising. Boots the Chemist, Timpson the Shoe Shop, The Light Bite: they are all here. Poorly dressed, depressed shoppers carrying cheap plastic bags abound, shuffling along as though unsure how to get through the interminable day.

Newsagents shops have fly-blown windows with ageing girls' comics (the comics, not the girls), old Beano annuals, plastic Korean-made bric-a-brac on tired display. The Galashiels Liberal Club – one fondly imagined it would be as smart and neat as David Steel and patronised by the chaps in the check shirts and green wellies – turns out to be a pub, selling incidentally William Younger's beer.

But if Peebles was smart and Selkirk was amusing, it wasn't only Galashiels which was depressing. Despite the surrounding scenery, which can be superb, there is something sad about the region. It is as though the Borderers don't really know who they are any more. As if they hardly know what their traditions are and can't be bothered trying to remember.

For the Borders ARE an anomaly in Scotland: perhaps being so removed from the developments in Scotland since the Highland clearance and the subsequent industrialisation has produced a limbo. Perhaps the Borders has spent its fury in its long struggle against the English. Perhaps there IS that complacency of which I had my suspicions before my visit.

Manhattan: island of my dreams *17th May 1980*

"I too walked the streets of Manhattan Island
and bathed in the waters round it,
I too felt the curious abrupt questionings
stir, within me."

Walt Whitman
'Crossing Brooklyn Ferry.'

'I like New York in June, how about you?' Arthur Freed, who wrote the song, also liked moonlight and motor trips, a Gershwin tune, and holding hands in the movie show when all the lights are low. And I like the song. It's got a feel to it, like you hear when Ella Fitzgerald sings of Manhattan, the Bronx and Staten. The romance of the song can't even be killed off for me by my regular rendering of it at parties. 'How About You' is not merely one of my party pieces, you see: it's one of the battle hymns of my Republic.

My Republic is smothered with a sticky romance, I'm afraid, for I am constantly trying to poke my everyday life into patterns I can understand, and those patterns are taken from the images of the movies. The images come from almost any time or period, though a lot depends on the last movie I've seen. In the 1900s it's all opera cloaks, gaslamps, and Raffles type figures. The twenties it's the bright young things, hipflasks, spats, and girls in green hats. But in the thirties and forties it's simply New York I think about. They are as fabled as the Arthurian legend to me, those times.

There's a vast Round Table, bigger than the one in the Algonquin Hotel, with Humphrey Bogart as Lancelot (the flawed seeker after truth/the Holy Grail), and Cole Porter as Roland, and all the other knights like Alan Ladd and Jimmy Cagney, Cary Grant, George Raft. There are the ladies fair like Carole Lombard and Myrna Loy and Margaret Sullavan and... I could go on for eight pages, and that's before I even touch the 1950s and sixties: my own decades, when I was a pimply youth. (Actually I never had any pimples as a youth. At least, not on the outside). New York, for me, is a touchstone, a lodestone. It is where I expect to find the Sword of Excalibur.

'My romance doesn't need a blue lagoon standing by...' Too

true it doesn't when it's got Central Park, Tiffany's, Schraft's, and 42nd Street. The Bowery, the garment district! Every time I look at my recently purchased map of the Big Apple a flush of wonderment goes through me, as though Tinkerbell has just cast fairy dust over me. I can't wait to stroll down Delancy Street or Lexington Avenue, and eat in diners, shoving down almost legendary delicacies such as blintzes and waffles, cups of java.

There are people around, though, who have to dampen this. They tell me that O. Henry's modern Baghdad is no more, and that the city is dying, it's ugly, you can't get around without being mugged. Mind you, they tell me the same thing about my own city, and they're the kind of people who'd be disappointed in Paris if they couldn't find Quasimodo nipping about among the pinnacles of Notre Dame. And they're the kind of people who could never understand why I feel the way I do about New York.

To try to explain this feeling of mine I have to tell you that I was born at the end of the War, you know THE War, the last one, not the Yom Kippur one or the one that lying cheating crook whom the British TV insists on interviewing says is going to be, or has been, the Third World War, but THE WAR. The world I grew up in, in Britain, was both cold, and suffocatingly cosy, all at the same time. And the first inkling that I had that the world could be larger than the fog-bound womb into which I was born came from a kind of general sense of America. Everything that was good, that had style, was American – tan shoes, Peggy Lee, American Cream Soda. I remember most of all, though, the Maxwell House coffee advert. It showed a massive panorama of Manhattan at night: a series of fairy lights in which enchanted beings lived, and walked the city streets, and underneath the picture it simply stated: 'Maxwell House – America's favourite coffee!' That was enough.

In any case, the violence, the danger of the street, is another part of the Big A's attraction. For in my vision of New York's romance I included the black wastelands too, those cities of endless and dreadful night in whose dark lanes the dead-end kids and their elder brothers played out their dramas. 'There are a thousand stories in The Naked City!', as the TV series used to say. The fly-boys and the spivs, the snap-brim men with their double-breasted suits and Kandinsky ties. Films ending with a narrator's intonation over a dead body in a mean alley – 'He died in the gutter where he belonged!'. All that was New York, too.

That worked alongside the glitter of High Society. This 'High Society' had little in common with the 'Haute Monde' of Britain or Europe. The British model was full of what New Yorkers called 'Hooray Henrys,' having pathetic cream teas while mouthing dialogue like: 'Oh! Geoffrey' Eh'm so unheppy!' Europeans, manwhile, had refugees when I was a child, and displaced persons and an intelligentsia who wrote novels about alienation, telling you about boredom by boring you half to death. But, back then, New York had clever, superficial people, who made epigrams out of a cocktail. 'Have you heard that Mimsie Starr, she got pinched in the Astor Bar. Well, Did you Evah!'. The Astor Bar – what a name for a boozer! One had highballs in the Astor Bar. I didn't know what a highball was, but I rather imagined it as a tall glass of bourbon with a pickled egg in it. The Ritz was ritzy. Cocktail bars had neon signs and canopies outside, and doormen in Ruritarian uniforms and hat-check girls. Broads came into such establishments dressed in their best friends and sat on high stools while barmen in white bumfreezer jackets shook – yes – a cocktail shaker, made of aluminium, in which they mixed Martinis and Manhattans and there was a Blue Lagoon standing by.

Hoagy Carmichael rolled his hands across the ivories, flicking cigarette ash into the cuspidor from time to time. Cole Porter could write a song in which he rhymed Mahatma Gandhi with Napoleon brandy. 'You're the tops!' he told a girl in the same song. The tops brandy, Gandhi, the cat's pyjamas.

Porter even ended this increasing apotheosis by telling the dame 'You're cellophane!'

During my childhood the American way had power and glamour and style. The Depression had long since gone, and the Stars and Stripes cast its shadow over every continent. And certainly over my own vision of Britain. There is a well-known photograph of London's Smithfield market taken in the early fifties. It sums up what Britain was like in those austere days. Men in greasy gabardine raincoats, women in headscarves, a thin drizzle ever-present, the yellow fog muzzling its nose against the window panes. In the industrial cities of the UK there was a seediness, an atmosphere of stale chip wrappers, and, at its most sinister, the rank air of 10 Rillington Place. But from the shores of Ikeland came brightness and gaiety, energy and excitement.

It is perhaps difficult for those of later generations than mine to see things that way. They were still at primary school, or even younger, when The Beatles, and British movies, and Swinging London was at its height. America had little to give at that time. A lot of those younger age groups had never seen an Alan Ladd film, or even heard of Cole Porter or Irving Berlin, or listened to Billie Holiday or swing bands. The world for them had maybe started in 1956 with rock 'n' roll, and had 'developed' into heavy rock and tattered jeans, Hare Krishna, hashish, and Hobbits. Some of this 'younger generation' talked as though Holywood had only ever made films which starred Jim Garner and Doris Day. Often enough they never quite perceived that, unknown to Miss Day, the scripts of such films were sometimes clever, subtle attacks on everything which Miss Blondie Butter stood for.

Indeed, the seventies generation even referred to those movies, those songs, those expressions of the American romance, as 'plastic' – meaning lacking in style. And that when a few years before style was, well, 'cellophane.'

Within the last five years or so we have, however, seen the emergence of a nostalgia boom. Whether or not it is actually

144

possible to re-create the so-called stability of the realisation of the American Dream of the Eisenhower years, when Junior threw the newspapers on to lost porches, and everybody had their teeth straightened, and still bear in mind the implications of the New Society, the upsurge of the blacks; the questioning of the American Puritan tradition, is a matter for the US politicians, such as they are, to find out, I suppose. Whether it is possible for 'style,' European, British, or transatlantic, to re-emerge is possibly an even more dubious question.

Certainly the sheer dreadfulness of the most of the art and entertainment forms of the last few years argues against this possibliity. We seem to be presently locked in a kind of Dark Ages of popular culture, in which the Morleyites hold increasing power. And if I sound a little misanthropic just now it is because these Morleyite answers grew up in my time. Because as a child I expected something better. As a child I wanted to wear a double-breasted white tuxedo and grow a thin moustache. I wanted to wear a panama hat and a white suit, get off the plane at Rio and have it off with Lauren Bacall in my hotel room to the whirr of the roof fans overhead, the light squinting through the blades of the venetian blinds. I couldn't wait for the new Cole Porters, the new Fred Astaires, the new New Yorkers.

Instead I have grown up into an age which seems to have worn the same pair of socks for far too long; which has piles of stale and dirty underwear lying about in its bedrooms. The image of New York for me was one which contained the glamour and glitter of High Society, as well as the 'social realism' of its back alleyways, the same back alleyways in which I was brought up myself, in the slums of that near-American city, Glasgow. I didn't use such images of New York as I saw in the Carlton Picture House in Townhead to escape from life, any more than I used torch songs or Hollywood musicals or Errol Flynn costume dramas to escape. I used New York as an image, in my head, to show me and explain to me what could be. To make me look over the rainbow. And I saw

145

More Bedside Urban Voltaire

the Maxwell House fairyland as having Marty and the dead-end kids and Bogart as well as Truman Capote, Holly Golightly and Mimsie Starr behind its window panes in these icons of skyscrapers. I waited for my place in that, my window pane, and now I find myself walking the streets of my Manhattan, only to discover that nobody lives there anymore.

People

Bulldogs 13th July 1990

I first met Winston face to face at Fuller's cake shop in Windsor when I was at Eton. Shortly after that I was elected to Pop: it was a momentous occasion in my long and distinguished life. What a splendid man Winston was. Little was I to know that, many years later, our British Bulldog would save the nation from the Nazis, Little was I to know that, later still, I would be able to write a collection of unctuous notes suggesting that I was possibly the greatest piece of absolute bloody rubbish what was never elected to the highest position in the land, though it was pretty high considering what a piece of bloody rubbish I have been all my life.

I well remember when I stood for election the first time. Oxford it was, I think. We Yooni chaps had our own seat, just for ourselves. I well remember how I argued – convincingly – that Mr Chamberlain was absolutely correct in giving in to Herr Hitler. After 50 years I have come up with a convincing rationale. We were not ready to take the Hun on. We didn't have enough Spitfires and the like. The Army wasn't ready. I myself belonged to the that group of decent chaps who insisted that we wouldn't be ready and I recollect spending many a happy hour among our sort of folk, who spent even more happy hours with senior Nazi officials and, in the end, it was all a great shame that we couldn't come to some sort of agreement with the Germans. After all, the autobahns were in full swing and there *were*, at the end of the day, a goodly few *Untermenschen* in our own sceptered isle.

What a fine mind I had. I was one of the few people in the country who could rattle off the odd strophe in classical Greek: the other was Enoch Powell. What a find mind Enoch Powell had. He was one of the few people who could toss off a racist diatribe in ancient Aramaic, and then become a Tory MP for the Irish Proddy Peasantry, and think that was okey-dokey. To

147

this day, I feel sure that a government headed by me and Enoch would have been able to give every aristocratic little creep in Britain a proper education and a peerage at the age of 12 and have closed the pits no bother with the miners still down them.

I am a patrician Tory and proud of it. What a victory it was when we beat the miners and killed lots of Argentinians. I look especially splendid in my wig and gown and all that stuff. I was born to it. My daddy was Lord Chancellor before me. I am a very religious man and a deeply committed Christian.

When I first met Winston face to face, little was I to know that here was another fine mind. What a coincidence it is to discover that very rich aristocrats seem somehow to possess all these fine minds and get to be in charge of everything. One of Winston's great virtues was his magnanimity. When we had luncheon together at the end of 1940 he said we must forgive the Germans after we beat them. I remember thinking how the Jews didn't seem to feel that unique quality of detachment to be a virtue at all; I don't know why. I thought it dashed decent of Winston, who knew my father well and had bought me a splendid cake in Fuller's when I was at Eton.

Winston's fall after Gallipoli was an enormous blessing in disguise. Classical scholars have often compared that disastrous military episode with the equally disastrous Sicilian expedition which was the decisive turning point against Athens in her famous war against Sparta . . . I can't keep this up. What a blessing-in-disguise Gallipoli was for my grandmother was very well disguised. Her husband – my grandfather – died there. On the same day, on the same beach, in the same regiment; his two brothers were killed as well. Their families, including my father's, never recovered from Winston's blessing in disguise, or his effing magnanimity either. Or the sheer bloody impertinence of Lord Hailsham in his latest autobiography.

I can take Norman Tebbit and his ilk.. Counter-jumpers like Heseltine. Oily little spivs like Parkinson, or harridans such as

Edwina Currie. I can even cope with my dislike of Margaret Hilda herself. Dislike is the word. They are the modern equivalents of the hard-faced men who did well out of the war. Give me a Hailsham and I will go along with Romanian-style executions. I would have piano-wire factories going full blast for this patrician scum. This is a different world from that in which I grew up; where I was told of the iniquities of Winston Churchill against the common people who fought so hard for democracy and under his remarkable leadership.

My dad told me Churchill did a grand job or us during the war. But never forget, he said. I thought I had. The recollections of that disgraceful old man, that fine mind, that aristo, that *Hailsham*, brought my father's injunction back. I would do it now, given the chance. I would have shot the bastard while he was gorging himself in Fuller's cake shop, and followed up with a bullet for Winnie to boot.

The Tallies   *27th October 1990*

I lived next door to a wee bloke called Allessandro Guiseppe Dimeo for years. He was known as Wee Alex. He spoke not a word of Italian and couldn't have made a spaghetti carbonara to save himself. In fact he couldn't have made much more than a bought fish supper. Actually he didn't. He ate fish suppers assiduously which he purchased from Mario's down at the corner of the street.

Mario couldn't speak English, let alone Italian. We are talking here of a level of assimilation which meant that only the name remained. Sometimes that didn't either. Wee Alex had an uncle who had changed the name "Dimeo" to "Dimes." Assimilation is a characteristic of Scotland's Italian community, and it has done it very well. The above examples of such a process are not unusual, but they are not entirely common either.

The sheer size of the Italo-Scots community is breathtaking. In the West of Scotland alone there are 17,000 people of Italian extraction. Everybody – especially those of the Roman Catholic religion – knows a Moscardini, a Pelosi, a Romano: we went to school with them. Italo-Scots have entered Scottish life, have penetrated the society, in such a way that it is impossible to imagine Scotland without a Moscardini, a Pelosi, a Romano. There are a lot more.

But the Italian community are a little more difficult to pin down than just the fact that all of us know people with an Italian Name. For a start they have been here a long time. There are more people of Italian extraction in Glasgow than anywhere else in Britain (though there are more Italians in Toronto, for instance, than there are in Milan: Italians are prolific immigrants). They came originally a long time ago to the United Kingdom.

But Scotland has to be different at all times from the rest of the UK. Go to Bedford and you will discover a thriving Italian community. They came to Britain from the south of Italy, from as far south as Sicily. They came to work in the brickworks, and they still do. When Italians first came to Scotland they crossed over to work in the building trades – showing their craft in terracotta tiling and in stucco for the exteriors of fine houses for the gentry. Even to this day you will find Italian craftsmen doing plasterwork in the restoration of country mansions. But the bulk of the Scottish Italians came across here at the turn of the century and after and from a different area of Italy and with different skills.

They came from the north, from Tuscany, from the deep poverty of feudality. They came in their droves from Provincia di Lucca, from Provincia di Cassino, from the Garfagnuina. From the lands around the river Sercchio, where the capital town was Castelnuovo – Newcastle in the English.

And they came to Scotland; a wet, canny land, with long winters and dour folk and the darkness of Presbyterianism enveloping them like fog. For the first Italian immigrants it must have been impossibly hard and dispiriting: they might have well as gone to the Russian steppes.

But the Italians worked hard when they came here and they

had the assistance of the Irish, in a strange way. Their Catholic faith, so alien to the Scottish environment prevailing in the late 1890s and for the next 40 years, allowed them to fix themselves into the Irish community in a way that could not be reciprocated by the Irish.

Nello Romano, a retired hairdresser from Glasgow says this: "The Irish got all the trouble about their religion. Hardly anybody noticed that we went to chapel too. We never got bothered in the same way. Until the war anyway."

We will get back to the war; meanwhile it is true what Nello said. The Irish took a great deal of sectarian trouble for nearly a century. Following on the heels of Highland immigration to the West of Scotland, the Irish came as strike-breakers, into the newly emerging jobs of an industrial revolution. For while the Irish took on occupations which directly competed with indigenous Scots, the Italians did no such thing.

They found – they invented – service occupations which had never existed in the dreich heartlands of central Scotland before. Fish and chip shops and hairdressers and ice cream parlours.

When Luigi Crolla first started out selling ice cream – gelati – little did he know what an industry he was starting up. A simple thing ice cream is, but an unashamed luxury it must have been to the Scots. From his wee barrow which he touted round the emerging seaside resorts of the Ayrshire coast came not only a national industry but a national institution: the café.

And from that dated the astonishing success of integration of the Italian community. For in the West of Scotland every street had a café at the corner. For some reason the Italian community has never been as sensitive as the Asian immigrants and while calling your corner store "The Pakki's" is often demurred at, to this day most Glaswegians call what was once a ubiquitous sight, an ice cream parlour, "the Tally's," Even Tallies call their shops by that name.

It is hard to understand how important these cafés were at

one time. Every West of Scotland person over the age of 35 could tell you. It was where you did your courting for a start. In Glasgow, you even did café crawls. The Bluebird, the 505, the Silver Slipper, the . . . listen; there isn't a one of us of my age who couldn't tell you of wonderful liaisons which occurred in Italian cafés.

There isn't one of us who didn't know an Italian café owner called Luigi or Giovanni or Luciano, and their bustling little wives called Maria or Lucia. And that is why there remains a deep sense of shame over what happened at the outbreak of the Second World War when the authorities roped up our Italians. And interned them.

They did too. People who had been here for 30 and more years; who were as much part of Scottish life as rain, found themselves taken into custody as aliens, as subversives, as potential traitors. It wasn't simply unfair, it was more than that. Not only were many of the Italian people of the Scottish community completely Scotticised, a lot of them were profoundly anti-fascist. It didn't matter: they got rounded up all the same.

On the east side of Scotland, many of them were interned for the entire duration: some died in the sinking of the Andorra Star. It was a shameful interlude in our history but, amazingly, Italo-Scots have borne little grudge. They remember though.

Marcella Evaristi, the Glasgow writer, remembered a little of it. Her family history recounts her uncles taken away at four in the morning in the clothes they stood up in and nothing else. Sy Sichi of the rather grand Unique fish restaurant in Glasgow remembers his father taken away in the night too. "He was in short trousers," he says, " and had been here since he was nine. Anyway he wasn't going to fight anyone at that age. Italians," he said engagingly, "didn't want to fight a fish supper." Been here is what the Italians say when they talk of Scotland. Here is where they intend to stay.

When I was at a wedding not so long ago there was Rosann Cherubini and her husband. You never saw more tartan in your life. You would have thought Rabbie Burns was getting married to his Bonny Jean.

When another friend of mine, Vincent Vezza – of impeccable Italian origin – was best man at a wedding he turned up in enough Balmorality to out-do Kenneth McKellar. The Italian community has integrated and tried harder than you can imagine and the internment during the last war of many Scottish Italians is something which we must be deeply ashamed of and for which we can hardly find words enough in apology.

Indeed Glaswegians were apologetic enough to have Sir Patrick Dollan – the famous Lord Provost of Glasgow in the war years – intercede on behalf of the community because everybody lived up the next close to a Mario and Lucia and couldn't believe the authorities would do such a thing. There are many Italo-Scots who will tell you of the blush in the cheeks of the big Highland polis who came to take Italian people away, and people they had known for over 20 years. The Italians of the east of Scotland were less prolific in number and had no such intercession made on their behalf by local politicos.

But the Italian community were better at their business than merely integrating. There are many Italians who lost their culture and their traditions.Some of them came back to their old ways too. Frank Pignatelli, director of education for Strathclyde, the largest education authority in Europe, returned to his own roots by rediscovering his language. But for many other people of Italian origin their roots have never left them. You ask many an Italian girl about the pressures put upon them to marry an Italian boy, preferably one in Italy itself; in the Old Country.

Ask them about the astonishing discipline which fathers made upon them – chaperones and in at nine at night at the age of 20 and obedience to the Church. Derek Rafaelli, a psychotherapist from Kirkcaldy now working in Glasgow, tells me of the time that his father actually tried to do an arranged marriage with the daughter of a friend from his own village in Barga.

Derek cooks Italian cuisine, and he speaks Italian too –

"Café Italian" he says, "Scottish Italian." (He does a grand rendition of Francie and Josie Tally-speak: Italians do it at will and find no contumely in it. When I spoke to the splendid 75-year-old Umberto di Marchi of the Queen's Café in Glasgow in Italian he replied in perfect cafetarian Glaswegian despite the fact that he is not only bilingual but can out-Glaswegian me as well. Scottish Italians like to take the mickey.) They also like to do good business. Just ask the proprietors of the Fazzi brothers' famous shop in Glasgow. Sando Sarti can speak Glaswegian with the best of us but he likes to sell Italy too.

But then, the Italians have done well in Scotland. Especially in the west. Listen to Derek Rafaelli again. "On the east coast there weren't so many of us and that was both a help and a hindrance. We didn't get much trouble because there were so few of us, but we didn't get as much acceptance for the same reason.

"And as a wee boy you don't want to be terribly different. There were times when I was embarrassed having my aunts and uncles in Italian in front of my pals. It was worse when you had to answer them back in our own tongue." Marcella Evaristi echoes this herself. As a child at the famous Notre-Dame school in Glasgow she frequently found herself feeling a stranger because of her definitely Italianate looks and the exoticism of her background. "You always felt you had to compensate in some way," she says. Well, she did. She became one of Scotland's best writers.

The same way that Rafaelli has become a prominent psychologist, and that Frank Pignatelli is the boss of education, and Osvaldo Francchi – Scotland's unofficial ambassador for the Italian community – is one of our best lawyers and that everybody called Coia is famous in this country.

Let met tell you a tale of a Coia. His name is Emilio, and he is the doyen of caricaturists. His old father announced one day that he was going to follow the dictum: "When in Rome do as the Romans do." Emilio tells the story with aplomb. "From a now on I'm a gonna drink a whisky witha my pasta," he told his astonished family. It hadn't occurred to him that where Italians drink their lovely wines with a meal the Scots do not generally throw down their national drink at tea-time. They drink tea. But Emilio's father was trying hard, as Italians in this country always have.

And they have tried hard and they have won. No group of immigrants has done better at it, not even the Highland immigrants who were my own forefathers. We brought our Calvinism, the Irish brought their peasant ways, and their fiery perverse love of language.

The Jews brought their European culture and philosophies, but also their clannishness. The Poles and Lithuanians and the Indians and Pakistanis and all the rest have come to Scotland to replace, in some ways, our own people who left over the last two centuries. But none have come to stay here and become Scottish as much as the Italians.

The Italians keep, in their own families, much of their language and their culture, their sense of themselves. But what a lot of class and style and – Godammit – fun they brought with them and to us. And they are us now as well.

Mum   *28th February 1986*

I remember once, a pal of mine telling me. Said a colleague thought I might have a private income. "Must have," said the colleague, "he wouldn't write such scurrilous stuff about his employers if he didn't have a few extra bob tucked away." My pal told him it was nothing but nonsense he had in his head. That I was a wee working-class sort of bloke. Lived in a council house.

The da had been a school janitor and I was by no means a scion of nobility and there was no safe hidden behind some family portrait and no spondulicks. A few weeks later my chum's colleague was utterly triumphant. "I told you that bloke was worth a fortune." he cried. "Look at it. It's in the paper. He says it himself. He employs servants." Big James, my pal, looks at my column of that day. There it is, in hard, cold print. "The domestic," it reads. The domestic which I employ. The lady who comes in and "does." A servant. James laughed till he damn near reached an embarrassing incontinence. For the domestic; the domestic I implied I employed was my mum.

I had rare fun with that. Used to irritate my mum; a bit anyway. She was proud of me and my column. I used to refer to her at all times as "the domestic." She certainly was my domestic if you took into consideration all the things she did for me. She did my washing. And ironing. I liked starch in my shirt collars. I wore collars so bound with Robin's solution I used to get cuts across the Adam's Apple which would have passed for suicide attempts. The woollens were positively bathed in Lenor.

Every time I stuck a pair of socks on, or pulled a sweater over my head, I used to hear a jingle, for God's sake. This is not to mention the ever-waiting grub which was there at two in the morning because I hadn't got home in time and had been down the pub instead and which my mum tried to keep reasonably hot with a tea-towel over the pot and all of that to no avail. She did a lot, mum, as a domestic. You see, she lived with me all these years.

All these years I have been calling her "the domestic" in my column. She got an occasional mention, that's true. "My mum agrees with me," I wrote once. I mentioned my mum perhaps 10, 11, times: I never told you her name. It was Mollie. Her real name was Beatrice, and I can't think of a name less like her than that. I don't know what a Beatrice should look like. But my mum was definitely a Mollie.

There were lots of famous Mollies back when she was a little girl – Mollie Allison comes to mind immediately – but my mum was not a Mollie like that. She was a small girl, with pink cheeks, and shyer than a girl has any right to be. She was brought up to be shy, timid, hard-working, and with such a sweet nature that the shyness would last for ever.

My mum was not a pushy sort of lady and she was so naive that she thought the best of everybody. She was sometimes astonished that people didn't square up to her own unreality about human nature. My mother thought so well of the world that nobody could have matched up to it. My mum died last Sunday, suddenly, and in a lot of pain. It was over quickly. At this moment I don't know how to write this, or even if I should.

All these years that my mum and I lived together: you get to know each other's ways. The worst thing about grief are the recriminations. Probably if I had died before my mum she'd have thought of some shirt still waiting to be pressed, or some other item she had left out. Of how she insisted in buying malt vinegar when I liked the acetic acid clear rubbish. It'd be something trivial like that.

She might have regretted some hapless argument which, in any case, I always won. But, of course, I didn't die before her, and I had tried to prepare myself for what was the most likely outcome of our long years together. I thought, often, at nights, even in idle moments during the day, of what it would be like when my mother made her final bow in this world. That was sort of the way I thought about it.

There is no preparation for this: Dear God, I wish right now, she was here. The recriminations are the worst part of it. I am trying very hard to put them out of my mind now, though they are real enough.

You think of a lot of things when somebody close to you dies. I can't get an image out of my head. I remember my mum when she was young. I remember a spring day when she walked me through the pine needles of that little wood which used to be in Linn Park. She was wearing a brown herringbone tweed suit. It had a curious brooch pinned to the lapel which I found when I was looking uselessly, through her papers. It was made out of two tiger claws and had a golden lion linking them, made out of yellow and red gold.

God knows why I remember my mother at that time, in that little wood. I think I recollect thinking then, when I was four years of age, that this was my mum, she was young, she wouldn't live for ever. Maybe I've just imagined that. I don't think so.

It is not the only image I have of my mother. I remember her fussing about you a million times with hankies, wiping imaginary specks of grime from your cheek.

I remember her polishing my damned shoes, for Heaven's sake, and bringing me a cup of tea while I lay abed of a Saturday morning. I remember me many a time with friends in the house and the whisky bottle playing even louder than the hi-fi, and my mother joining in and Leo and Tam and Sandy and John and so many of my friends who became her friends getting her up to dance a foxtrot which they couldn't do really and my mother showing them the footsteps.

As I write this, the funeral is tomorrow: I don't want to go: I'm not sure I can face all that grief. My own is hard enough to bear. I wish, above all else, I had thought to write about my mum before, when she was alive. She was proud of me and my column. But not, surely not, as proud as I am of her.